AF454144

Art of Public Speaking

J. Berg Esenwein; Dale Carnegie

PAGES PLANET PUBLISHING

Published by

PAGES PLANET PUBLISHING 

Email: pagesplanetpublishing@gmail.com

For details or inquiries, please reach out to the publisher at the email above.

First published by Pages Planet Publishing in 2024

Title: Art of public speaking by Dale Carnegie

Paperback ISBN: 9789361904967

Hardback ISBN: 9789361902505

Ebook ISBN: 9789361909399

Things To Think Of First.
A Foreword

The efficiency of a book is like that of a man, in one important respect: its attitude toward its subject is the first source of its power. A book may be full of good ideas well expressed, but if its writer views his subject from the wrong angle even his excellent advice may prove to be ineffective.

This book stands or falls by its authors' attitude toward its subject. If the best way to teach oneself or others to speak effectively in public is to fill the mind with rules, and to set up fixed standards for the interpretation of thought, the utterance of language, the making of gestures, and all the rest, then this book will be limited in value to such stray ideas throughout its pages as may prove helpful to the reader— as an effort to enforce a group of principles it must be reckoned a failure, because it is then untrue.

It is of some importance, therefore, to those who take up this volume with open mind that they should see clearly at the out–start what is the thought that at once underlies and is builded through this structure. In plain words it is this:

Training in public speaking is not a matter of externals—primarily; it is not a matter of imitation—fundamentally; it is not a matter of conformity to standards—at all. Public speaking is public utterance, public issuance, of the man himself; therefore the first thing both in time and in importance is that the man should be and think and feel things that are worthy of being given forth. Unless there be something of value within, no tricks of training can ever make of the talker anything more than a machine—albeit a highly perfected machine—for the delivery of other men's goods. So self–development is fundamental in our plan.

The second principle lies close to the first: The man must enthrone his will to rule over his thought, his feelings, and all his physical powers, so that the outer self may give perfect, unhampered expression to the inner. It is futile, we assert, to lay down systems of rules for voice culture, intonation, gesture, and what not, unless these two principles of having something to say and making the will sovereign have at least begun to make themselves felt in the life.

The third principle will, we surmise, arouse no dispute: No one can learn *how* to speak who does not first speak as best he can. That may seem like a vicious circle in statement, but it will bear examination.

Many teachers have begun with the *how*. Vain effort! It is an ancient truism that we learn to do by doing. The first thing for the beginner in public speaking is to speak—not to study voice and gesture and the rest. Once he has spoken he can improve himself by self–observation or according to the criticisms of those who hear.

But how shall he be able to criticise himself? Simply by finding out three things: What are the qualities which by common consent go to make up an effective speaker; by what means at least some of these qualities may be acquired; and what wrong habits of speech in himself work against his acquiring and using the qualities which he finds to be good.

Experience, then, is not only the best teacher, but the first and the last. But experience must be a dual thing—the experience of others must be used to supplement, correct and justify our own experience; in this way we shall become our own best critics only after we have trained ourselves in self–knowledge, the knowledge of what other minds think, and in the ability to judge ourselves by the standards we have come to believe are right. "If I ought," said Kant, "I can."

An examination of the contents of this volume will show how consistently these articles of faith have been declared, expounded, and illustrated. The student is urged to begin to speak at once of what he knows. Then he is given simple suggestions for self–control, with gradually increasing emphasis upon the power of the inner man over the outer. Next, the way to the rich storehouses of material is pointed out. And finally, all the while he is urged to speak, *speak, SPEAK* as he is applying to his own methods, in his own *personal* way, the principles he has gathered from his own experience and observation and the recorded experiences of others.

So now at the very first let it be as clear as light that methods are secondary matters; that the full mind, the warm heart, the dominant will are primary—and not only primary but paramount; for unless it be a full being that uses the methods it will be like dressing a wooden image in the clothes of a man.

J. BERG ESENWEIN. NARBERTH, PA., JANUARY 1, 1915.

Epigraph

Sense never fails to give them that have it, Words enough to make them understood. It too often happens in some conversations, as in Apothecary Shops, that those Pots that are Empty, or have Things of small Value in them, are as gaudily Dress'd as those that are full of precious Drugs.

They that soar too high, often fall hard, making a low and level Dwelling preferable. The tallest Trees are most in the Power of the Winds, and Ambitious Men of the Blasts of Fortune. Buildings have need of a good Foundation, that lie so much exposed to the Weather.

—WILLIAM PENN.

1. Acquiring Confidence Before An Audience

There is a strange sensation often experienced in the presence of an audience. It may proceed from the gaze of the many eyes that turn upon the speaker, especially if he permits himself to steadily return that gaze. Most speakers have been conscious of this in a nameless thrill, a real something, pervading the atmosphere, tangible, evanescent, indescribable. All writers have borne testimony to the power of a speaker's eye in impressing an audience. This influence which we are now considering is the reverse of that picture—the power *their* eyes may exert upon him, especially before he begins to speak: after the inward fires of oratory are fanned into flame the eyes of the audience lose all terror.

—*WILLIAM PITTENGER, Extempore Speech.*

Students of public speaking continually ask, "How can I overcome self–consciousness and the fear that paralyzes me before an audience?"

Did you ever notice in looking from a train window that some horses feed near the track and never even pause to look up at the thundering cars, while just ahead at the next railroad crossing a farmer's wife will be nervously trying to quiet her scared horse as the train goes by?

How would you cure a horse that is afraid of cars—graze him in a back–woods lot where he would never see steam–engines or automobiles, or drive or pasture him where he would frequently see the machines?

Apply horse–sense to ridding yourself of self–consciousness and fear: face an audience as frequently as you can, and you will soon stop shying. You can never attain freedom from stage–fright by reading a treatise. A book may give you excellent suggestions on how best to conduct yourself in the water, but sooner or later you must get wet, perhaps even strangle and be "half scared to death." There are a great many "wetless" bathing suits worn at the seashore, but no one ever learns to swim in them. To plunge is the only way.

Practise, *practise, PRACTISE* in speaking before an audience will tend to remove all fear of audiences, just as practise in swimming will lead to confidence and facility in the water. You must learn to speak by speaking.

The Apostle Paul tells us that every man must work out his own salvation. All we can do here is to offer you suggestions as to how best to prepare for your plunge. The real plunge no one can take for you. A doctor may prescribe, but *you* must take the medicine.

Do not be disheartened if at first you suffer from stage–fright. Dan Patch was more susceptible to suffering than a superannuated dray horse would be. It never hurts a fool to appear before an audience, for his capacity is not a capacity for feeling. A blow that would kill a civilized man soon heals on a savage. The higher we go in the scale of life, the greater is the capacity for suffering.

For one reason or another, some master–speakers never entirely overcome stage–fright, but it will pay you to spare no pains to conquer it. Daniel Webster failed in his first appearance and had to take his seat without finishing his speech because he was nervous. Gladstone was often troubled with self–consciousness in the beginning of an address. Beecher was always perturbed before talking in public.

Blacksmiths sometimes twist a rope tight around the nose of a horse, and by thus inflicting a little pain they distract his attention from the shoeing process. One way to get air out of a glass is to pour in water.

Be Absorbed by Your Subject

Apply the blacksmith's homely principle when you are speaking. If you feel deeply about your subject you will be able to think of little else. Concentration is a process of distraction from less important matters. It is too late to think about the cut of your coat when once you are upon the platform, so centre your interest on what you are about to say—fill your mind with your speech–material and, like the infilling water in the glass, it will drive out your unsubstantial fears.

Self-consciousness is undue consciousness of self, and, for the purpose of delivery, self is secondary to your subject, not only in the opinion of the audience, but, if you are wise, in your own. To hold any other view is to regard yourself as an exhibit instead of as a messenger with a message worth delivering. Do you remember Elbert Hubbard's tremendous little tract, "A Message to Garcia"? The youth subordinated himself to the message he bore. So must you, by all the determination you can muster. It is sheer egotism to fill your mind with thoughts of self when a greater thing is there—*TRUTH*. Say this to yourself sternly, and shame your self-consciousness into quiescence. If the theater caught fire you could rush to the stage and shout directions to the audience without any self-consciousness, for the importance of what you were saying would drive all fear-thoughts out of your mind.

Far worse than self-consciousness through fear of doing poorly is self-consciousness through assumption of doing well. The first sign of greatness is when a man does not attempt to look and act great. Before you can call yourself a man at all, Kipling assures us, you must "not look too good nor talk too wise."

Nothing advertises itself so thoroughly as conceit. One may be so full of self as to be empty. Voltaire said, "We must conceal self-love." But that can not be done. You know this to be true, for you have recognized overweening self-love in others. If you have it, others are seeing it in you. There are things in this world bigger than self, and in working for them self will be forgotten, or—what is better—remembered only so as to help us win toward higher things.

Have Something to Say

The trouble with many speakers is that they go before an audience with their minds a blank. It is no wonder that nature, abhorring a vacuum, fills them with the nearest thing handy, which generally happens to be, "I wonder if I am doing this right! How does my hair look? I know I shall fail." Their prophetic souls are sure to be right.

It is not enough to be absorbed by your subject—to acquire self-confidence you must have something in which to be confident. If you go before an audience without any preparation, or previous knowledge of your subject, you ought to be self-conscious—you ought to be ashamed to steal the time of your audience. Prepare yourself. Know what you are going to talk about, and, in general, how you are going to say it. Have the first few sentences worked out completely so that you may not be troubled in the beginning to find words. Know your subject better than your hearers know it, and you have nothing to fear.

After Preparing for Success, Expect It

Let your bearing be modestly confident, but most of all be modestly confident within. Over–confidence is bad, but to tolerate premonitions of failure is worse, for a bold man may win attention by his very bearing, while a rabbit–hearted coward invites disaster.

Humility is not the personal discount that we must offer in the presence of others—against this old interpretation there has been a most healthy modern reaction. True humility any man who thoroughly knows himself must feel; but it is not a humility that assumes a worm–like meekness; it is rather a strong, vibrant prayer for greater power for service—a prayer that Uriah Heep could never have uttered.

Washington Irving once introduced Charles Dickens at a dinner given in the latter's honor. In the middle of his speech Irving hesitated, became embarrassed, and sat down awkwardly. Turning to a friend beside him he remarked, "There, I told you I would fail, and I did."

If you believe you will fail, there is no hope for you. You will.

Rid yourself of this I–am–a–poor–worm–in–the–dust idea. You are a god, with infinite capabilities. "All things are ready if the mind be so." The eagle looks the cloudless sun in the face.

Assume Mastery Over Your Audience

In public speech, as in electricity, there is a positive and a negative force. Either you or your audience are going to possess the positive factor. If you assume it you can almost invariably make it yours. If you assume the negative you are sure to be negative. Assuming a virtue or a vice vitalizes it. Summon all your power of self–direction, and remember that though your audience is infinitely more important than you, the truth is more important than both of you, because it is eternal. If your mind falters in its leadership the sword will drop from your hands. Your assumption of being able to instruct or lead or inspire a multitude or even a small group of people may appall you as being colossal impudence—as indeed it may be; but having once essayed to speak, be courageous. *BE* courageous—it lies within you to be what you will. *MAKE* yourself be calm and confident.

Reflect that your audience will not hurt you. If Beecher in Liverpool had spoken behind a wire screen he would have invited the audience to throw the over-ripe missiles with which they were loaded; but he was a man, confronted his hostile hearers fearlessly—and won them.

In facing your audience, pause a moment and look them over—a hundred chances to one they want you to succeed, for what man is so foolish as to spend his time, perhaps his money, in the hope that you will waste his investment by talking dully?

Concluding Hints

Do not make haste to begin—haste shows lack of control.

Do not apologize. It ought not to be necessary; and if it is, it will not help. Go straight ahead.

Take a deep breath, relax, and begin in a quiet conversational tone as though you were speaking to one large friend. You will not find it half so bad as you imagined; really, it is like taking a cold plunge: after you are in, the water is fine. In fact, having spoken a few times you will even anticipate the plunge with exhilaration. To stand before an audience and make them think your thoughts after you is one of the greatest pleasures you can ever know. Instead of fearing it, you ought to be as anxious as the fox hounds straining at their leashes, or the race horses tugging at their reins.

So cast out fear, for fear is cowardly—when it is not mastered. The bravest know fear, but they do not yield to it. Face your audience pluckily—if your knees quake, *MAKE* them stop. In your audience lies some victory for you and the cause you represent. Go win it. Suppose Charles Martell had been afraid to hammer the Saracen at Tours; suppose Columbus had feared to venture out into the unknown West; suppose our forefathers had been too timid to oppose the tyranny of George the Third; suppose that any man who ever did anything worth while had been a coward! The world owes its progress to the men who have dared, and you must dare to speak the effective word that is in your heart to speak—for often it requires courage to utter a single sentence. But remember that men erect no monuments and weave no laurels for those who fear to do what they can.

Is all this unsympathetic, do you say?

Man, what you need is not sympathy, but a push. No one doubts that temperament and nerves and illness and even praiseworthy modesty may, singly or combined, cause the speaker's cheek to blanch before an audience, but neither can any one doubt that coddling will magnify this weakness. The victory lies in a fearless frame of mind. Prof. Walter Dill Scott says: "Success or failure in business is caused more by mental attitude even than by mental capacity." Banish the fear–attitude; acquire the confident attitude. And remember that the only way to acquire it is—*to acquire it.*

In this foundation chapter we have tried to strike the tone of much that is to follow. Many of these ideas will be amplified and enforced in a more specific way; but through all these chapters on an art which Mr. Gladstone believed to be more powerful than the public press, the note of *justifiable self–confidence* must sound again and again.

QUESTIONS AND EXERCISES.

1. What is the cause of self–consciousness?

2. Why are animals free from it?

3. What is your observation regarding self–consciousness in children?

4. Why are you free from it under the stress of unusual excitement?

5. How does moderate excitement affect you?

6. What are the two fundamental requisites for the acquiring of self–confidence? Which is the more important?

7. What effect does confidence on the part of the speaker have on the audience?

8. Write out a two–minute speech on "Confidence and Cowardice."

9. What effect do habits of thought have on confidence? In this connection read the chapter on "Right Thinking and Personality."

10. Write out very briefly any experience you may have had involving the teachings of this chapter.

11. Give a three-minute talk on "Stage-Fright," including a (kindly) imitation of two or more victims.

2. The Sin Of Monotony

One day Ennui was born from Uniformity.

—MOTTE.

Our English has changed with the years so that many words now connote more than they did originally. This is true of the word *monotonous*. From "having but one tone," it has come to mean more broadly, "lack of variation."

The monotonous speaker not only drones along in the same volume and pitch of tone but uses always the same emphasis, the same speed, the same thoughts—or dispenses with thought altogether.

Monotony, the cardinal and most common sin of the public speaker, is not a transgression—it is rather a sin of omission, for it consists in living up to the confession of the Prayer Book: "We have left undone those things we ought to have done."

Emerson says, "The virtue of art lies in detachment, in sequestering one object from the embarrassing variety." That is just what the monotonous speaker fails to do—he does *not* detach one thought or phrase from another, they are all expressed in the same manner.

To tell you that your speech is monotonous may mean very little to you, so let us look at the nature—and the curse—of monotony in other spheres of life, then we shall appreciate more fully how it will blight an otherwise good speech.

If the Victrola in the adjoining apartment grinds out just three selections over and over again, it is pretty safe to assume that your neighbor has no other records. If a speaker uses only a few of his powers, it points very plainly to the fact that the rest of his powers are not developed. Monotony reveals our limitations.

In its effect on its victim, monotony is actually deadly—it will drive the bloom from the cheek and the lustre from the eye as quickly as sin, and often leads to viciousness. The worst punishment that human ingenuity has ever been able to invent is extreme monotony—solitary confinement. Lay a marble on the table and do nothing eighteen hours of the day but change that marble from one point to another and back again, and you will go insane if you continue long enough.

So this thing that shortens life, and is used as the most cruel of punishments in our prisons, is the thing that will destroy all the life and force of a speech. Avoid it as you would shun a deadly dull bore. The "idle rich" can have half–a–dozen homes, command all the varieties of foods gathered from the four corners of the earth, and sail for Africa or Alaska at their pleasure; but the poverty–stricken man must walk or take a street car—he does not have the choice of yacht, auto, or special train. He must spend the most of his life in labor and be content with the staples of the food–market. Monotony is poverty, whether in speech or in life. Strive to increase the variety of your speech as the business man labors to augment his wealth.

Bird–songs, forest glens, and mountains are not monotonous—it is the long rows of brown–stone fronts and the miles of paved streets that are so terribly same. Nature in her wealth gives us endless variety; man with his limitations is often monotonous. Get back to nature in your methods of speech–making.

The power of variety lies in its pleasure–giving quality. The great truths of the world have often been couched in fascinating stories - "Les Miserables," for instance. If you wish to teach or influence men, you must please them, first or last. Strike the same note on the piano over and over again. This will give you some idea of the displeasing, jarring effect monotony has on the ear. The dictionary defines "monotonous" as being synonymous with "wearisome." That is putting it mildly. It is maddening. The department–store prince does not disgust the public by playing only the one tune, "Come Buy My Wares!" He gives recitals on a $125,000 organ, and the pleased people naturally slip into a buying mood.

How to Conquer Monotony

We obviate monotony in dress by replenishing our wardrobes. We avoid monotony in speech by multiplying our powers of speech. We multiply our powers of speech by increasing our tools.

The carpenter has special implements with which to construct the several parts of a building. The organist has certain keys and stops which he manipulates to produce his harmonies and effects. In like manner the speaker has certain instruments and tools at his command by which he builds his argument, plays on the feelings, and guides the beliefs of his audience. To give you a conception of these instruments, and practical help in learning to use them, are the purposes of the immediately following chapters.

Why did not the Children of Israel whirl through the desert in limousines, and why did not Noah have moving–picture entertainments and talking machines on the Ark? The laws that enable us to operate an automobile, produce moving–pictures, or music on the Victrola, would have worked just as well then as they do today. It was ignorance of law that for ages deprived humanity of our modern conveniences. Many speakers still use ox–cart methods in their speech instead of employing automobile or overland–express methods. They are ignorant of laws that make for efficiency in speaking. Just to the extent that you regard and use the laws that we are about to examine and learn how to use will you have efficiency and force in your speaking; and just to the extent that you disregard them will your speaking be feeble and ineffective. We cannot impress too thoroughly upon you the necessity for a real working mastery of these principles. They are the very foundations of successful speaking. "Get your principles right," said Napoleon, "and the rest is a matter of detail."

It is useless to shoe a dead horse, and all the sound principles in Christendom will never make a live speech out of a dead one. So let it be understood that public speaking is not a matter of mastering a few dead rules; the most important law of public speech is the necessity for truth, force, feeling, and life. Forget all else, but not this.

When you have mastered the mechanics of speech outlined in the next few chapters you will no longer be troubled with monotony. The complete knowledge of these principles and the ability to apply them will give you great variety in your powers of expression. But they cannot be mastered and applied by thinking or reading about them—you must practise, *practise, PRACTISE.* If no one else will listen to you, listen to yourself—you must always be your own best critic, and the severest one of all.

The technical principles that we lay down in the following chapters are not arbitrary creations of our own. They are all founded on the practices that good speakers and actors adopt—either naturally and unconsciously or under instruction—in getting their effects.

It is useless to warn the student that he must be natural. To be natural may be to be monotonous. The little strawberry up in the arctics with a few tiny seeds and an acid tang is a natural berry, but it is not to be compared with the improved variety that we enjoy here. The dwarfed oak on the rocky hillside is natural, but a poor thing compared with the beautiful tree found in the rich, moist bottom lands. Be natural— but improve your natural gifts until you have approached the ideal, for we must strive after idealized nature, in fruit, tree, and speech.

QUESTIONS AND EXERCISES.

1. What are the causes of monotony?

2. Cite some instances in nature.

3. Cite instances in man's daily life.

4. Describe some of the effects of monotony in both cases.

5. Read aloud some speech without paying particular attention to its meaning or force.

6. Now repeat it after you have thoroughly assimilated its matter and spirit. What difference do you notice in its rendition?

7. Why is monotony one of the worst as well as one of the most common faults of speakers?

3. Efficiency Through Emphasis And Subordination

In a word, the principle of emphasis...is followed best, not by remembering particular rules, but by being full of a particular feeling.

—C.S. BALDWIN, *Writing and Speaking*.

The gun that scatters too much does not bag the birds. The same principle applies to speech. The speaker that fires his force and emphasis at random into a sentence will not get results. Not every word is of special importance—therefore only certain words demand emphasis.

You say Massa*CHU*setts and Minne*AP*olis, you do not emphasize each syllable alike, but hit the accented syllable with force and hurry over the unimportant ones. Now why do you not apply this principle in speaking a sentence? To some extent you do, in ordinary speech; but do you in public discourse? It is there that monotony caused by lack of emphasis is so painfully apparent.

So far as emphasis is concerned, you may consider the average sentence as just one big word, with the important word as the accented syllable. Note the following:

"Destiny is not a matter of chance. It is a matter of choice."

You might as well say *MASS–A–CHU–SETTS*, emphasizing every syllable equally, as to lay equal stress on each word in the foregoing sentences.

Speak it aloud and see. Of course you will want to emphasize *destiny*, for it is the principal idea in your declaration, and you will put some emphasis on *not*, else your hearers may think you are affirming that destiny *is* a matter of chance. By all means you must emphasize *chance*, for it is one of the two big ideas in the statement.

Another reason why *chance* takes emphasis is that it is contrasted with *choice* in the next sentence. Obviously, the author has contrasted these ideas purposely, so that they might be more emphatic, and here we see that contrast is one of the very first devices to gain emphasis.

As a public speaker you can assist this emphasis of contrast with your voice. If you say, "My horse is not *black*," what color immediately comes into mind? White, naturally, for that is the opposite of black. If you wish to bring out the thought that destiny is a matter of choice, you can do so more effectively by first saying that *"DESTINY is NOT a matter of CHANCE."* Is not the color of the horse impressed upon us more emphatically when you say, "My horse is *NOT BLACK*. He is *WHITE"* than it would be by hearing you assert merely that your horse is white?

In the second sentence of the statement there is only one important word—*choice*. It is the one word that positively defines the quality of the subject being discussed, and the author of those lines desired to bring it out emphatically, as he has shown by contrasting it with another idea. These lines, then, would read like this:

"DESTINY is *NOT* a matter of *CHANCE.* It is a matter of *CHOICE."* Now read this over, striking the words in capitals with a great deal of force.

In almost every sentence there are a few *MOUNTAIN PEAK WORDS* that represent the big, important ideas. When you pick up the evening paper you can tell at a glance which are the important news articles. Thanks to the editor, he does not tell about a "hold up" in Hong Kong in the same sized type as he uses to report the death of five firemen in your home city. Size of type is his device to show emphasis in bold relief. He brings out sometimes even in red headlines the striking news of the day.

It would be a boon to speech–making if speakers would conserve the attention of their audiences in the same way and emphasize only the words representing the important ideas. The average speaker will deliver the foregoing line on destiny with about the same amount of emphasis on each word. Instead of saying, "It is a matter of *CHOICE,"* he will deliver it, "It is a matter of choice," or *"IT IS A MATTER OF CHOICE"*—both equally bad.

Charles Dana, the famous editor of *The New York Sun*, told one of his reporters that if he went up the street and saw a dog bite a man, to pay no attention to it. *The Sun* could not afford to waste the time and attention of its readers on such unimportant happenings. "But," said

Mr. Dana, "if you see a man bite a dog, hurry back to the office and write the story." Of course that is news; that is unusual.

Now the speaker who says "*IT IS A MATTER OF CHOICE*" is putting too much emphasis upon things that are of no more importance to metropolitan readers than a dog bite, and when he fails to emphasize "choice" he is like the reporter who "passes up" the man's biting a dog. The ideal speaker makes his big words stand out like mountain peaks; his unimportant words are submerged like stream–beds. His big thoughts stand like huge oaks; his ideas of no especial value are merely like the grass around the tree.

From all this we may deduce this important principle: *EMPHASIS* is a matter of *CONTRAST* and *COMPARISON*.

Recently the *New York American* featured an editorial by Arthur Brisbane. Note the following, printed in the same type as given here.

=We do not know what the President THOUGHT when he got that message, or what the elephant thinks when he sees the mouse, but we do know what the President DID.=

The words *THOUGHT* and *DID* immediately catch the reader's attention because they are different from the others, not especially because they are larger. If all the rest of the words in this sentence were made ten times as large as they are, and *DID* and *THOUGHT* were kept at their present size, they would still be emphatic, because different.

Take the following from Robert Chambers' novel, "The Business of Life." The words *you*, *had*, *would*, are all emphatic, because they have been made different.

He looked at her in angry astonishment.

"Well, what do *you* call it if it isn't cowardice—to slink off and marry a defenseless girl like that!"

"Did you expect me to give you a chance to destroy me and poison Jacqueline's mind? If I *had* been guilty of the thing with which you charge me, what I have done *would* have been cowardly. Otherwise, it is justified."

A Fifth Avenue bus would attract attention up at Minisink Ford, New York, while one of the ox teams that frequently pass there would attract attention on Fifth Avenue. To make a word emphatic, deliver it differently from the manner in which the words surrounding it are delivered. If you have been talking loudly, utter the emphatic word in a concentrated whisper—and you have intense emphasis. If you have been going fast, go very slow on the emphatic word. If you have been talking on a low pitch, jump to a high one on the emphatic word. If you have been talking on a high pitch, take a low one on your emphatic ideas. Read the chapters on "Inflection," "Feeling," "Pause," "Change of Pitch," "Change of Tempo." Each of these will explain in detail how to get emphasis through the use of a certain principle.

In this chapter, however, we are considering only one form of emphasis: that of applying force to the important word and subordinating the unimportant words. Do not forget: this is one of the main methods that you must continually employ in getting your effects.

Let us not confound loudness with emphasis. To yell is not a sign of earnestness, intelligence, or feeling. The kind of force that we want applied to the emphatic word is not entirely physical. True, the emphatic word may be spoken more loudly, or it may be spoken more softly, but the *real* quality desired is intensity, earnestness. It must come from within, outward.

Last night a speaker said: "The curse of this country is not a lack of education. It's politics." He emphasized *curse, lack, education, politics.* The other words were hurried over and thus given no comparative importance at all. The word *politics* was flamed out with great feeling as he slapped his hands together indignantly. His emphasis was both correct and powerful. He concentrated all our attention on the words that meant something, instead of holding it up on such words as *of this, a, of, It's.*

What would you think of a guide who agreed to show New York to a stranger and then took up his time by visiting Chinese laundries and boot-blacking "parlors" on the side streets? There is only one excuse for a speaker's asking the attention of his audience: He must have either truth or entertainment for them. If he wearies their attention with trifles they will have neither vivacity nor desire left when he reaches words of Wall-Street and skyscraper importance. You do not dwell on these small words in your everyday conversation, because you are not a conversational bore. Apply the correct method of everyday speech to the platform. As we have noted elsewhere, public speaking is very much like conversation enlarged.

Sometimes, for big emphasis, it is advisable to lay stress on every single syllable in a word, as *absolutely* in the following sentence:

I ab–so–lute–ly refuse to grant your demand.

Now and then this principle should be applied to an emphatic sentence by stressing each word. It is a good device for exciting special attention, and it furnishes a pleasing variety. Patrick Henry's notable climax could be delivered in that manner very effectively: "Give—me—liberty—or—give—me—death." The italicized part of the following might also be delivered with this every–word emphasis. Of course, there are many ways of delivering it; this is only one of several good interpretations that might be chosen.

Knowing the price we must pay, the sacrifice we must make, the burdens we must carry, the assaults we must endure—knowing full well the cost—yet we enlist, and we enlist for the war. For we know the justice of our cause, and *we know, too, its certain triumph.*

—*From "Pass Prosperity Around," by* ALBERT J. BEVERIDGE, *before the Chicago National Convention of the Progressive Party.*

Strongly emphasizing a single word has a tendency to suggest its antithesis. Notice how the meaning changes by merely putting the emphasis on different words in the following sentence. The parenthetical expressions would really not be needed to supplement the emphatic words.

I intended to buy a house this Spring (even if you did not).

I *INTENDED* to buy a house this Spring (but something prevented).

I intended to *BUY* a house this Spring (instead of renting as heretofore).

I intended to buy a *HOUSE* this Spring (and not an automobile).

I intended to buy a house *THIS* Spring (instead of next Spring).

I intended to buy a house this *SPRING* (instead of in the Autumn).

When a great battle is reported in the papers, they do not keep emphasizing the same facts over and over again. They try to get new information, or a "new slant." The news that takes an important place in the morning edition will be relegated to a small space in the late afternoon edition. We are interested in new ideas and new facts. This principle has a very important bearing in determining your emphasis. Do not emphasize the same idea over and over again unless you desire to lay extra stress on it; Senator Thurston desired to put the maximum amount of emphasis on "force" in his speech on page 50. Note how force is emphasized repeatedly. As a general rule, however, the new idea, the "new slant," whether in a newspaper report of a battle or a speaker's enunciation of his ideas, is emphatic.

In the following selection, "larger" is emphatic, for it is the new idea. All men have eyes, but this man asks for a *LARGER* eye.

This man with the larger eye says he will discover, not rivers or safety appliances for aeroplanes, but *NEW STARS* and *SUNS*. "New stars and suns" are hardly as emphatic as the word "larger." Why? Because we expect an astronomer to discover heavenly bodies rather than cooking recipes. The words, "Republic needs" in the next sentence, are emphatic; they introduce a new and important idea. Republics have always needed men, but the author says they need *NEW* men. "New" is emphatic because it introduces a new idea. In like manner, "soil," "grain," "tools," are also emphatic.

The most emphatic words are italicized in this selection. Are there any others you would emphasize? Why?

The old astronomer said, "Give me a *larger* eye, and I will discover *new stars* and *suns*." That is what the *republic needs* today—*new men*—men who are *wise* toward the *soil*, toward the *grains*, toward the *tools*. If God would only raise up for the people two or three men like *Watt, Fulton* and *McCormick*, they would be *worth more* to the *State* than that *treasure box* named *California* or *Mexico*. And the *real supremacy* of man is based upon his *capacity* for *education*. Man is *unique* in the *length* of his *childhood*, which means the *period* of *plasticity* and *education*. The childhood of a *moth*, the distance that stands between the hatching of the *robin* and its *maturity*, represent a *few hours* or a *few weeks*, but *twenty years* for growth stands between *man's* cradle and his citizenship. This protracted childhood makes it possible to hand over to the boy all the *accumulated stores achieved* by *races* and *civilizations* through *thousands* of *years.*

—Anonymous.

You must understand that there are no steel–riveted rules of emphasis. It is not always possible to designate which word must, and which must not be emphasized. One speaker will put one interpretation on a speech, another speaker will use different emphasis to bring out a different interpretation. No one can say that one interpretation is right and the other wrong. This principle must be borne in mind in all our marked exercises. Here your own intelligence must guide—and greatly to your profit.

QUESTIONS AND EXERCISES.

1. What is emphasis?

2. Describe one method of destroying monotony of thought–presentation.

3. What relation does this have to the use of the voice?

4. Which words should be emphasized, which subordinated, in a sentence?

5. Read the selections on pages 50, 51, 52, 53 and 54, devoting special attention to emphasizing the important words or phrases and subordinating the unimportant ones. Read again, changing emphasis slightly. What is the effect?

6. Read some sentence repeatedly, emphasizing a different word each time, and show how the meaning is changed, as is done on page 22.

7. What is the effect of a lack of emphasis?

8. Read the selections on pages 30 and 48, emphasizing every word. What is the effect on the emphasis?

9. When is it permissible to emphasize every single word in a sentence?

10. Note the emphasis and subordination in some conversation or speech you have heard. Were they well made? Why? Can you suggest any improvement?

11. From a newspaper or a magazine, clip a report of an address, or a biographical eulogy. Mark the passage for emphasis and bring it with you to class.

12. In the following passage, would you make any changes in the author's markings for emphasis? Where? Why? Bear in mind that not all words marked require the same *degree* of emphasis—*in a wide variety of emphasis, and in nice shading of the gradations, lie the excellence of emphatic speech.*

I would call him *Napoleon*, but Napoleon made his way to empire over *broken oaths* and through a *sea* of *blood*. This man *never* broke his word. "No Retaliation" was his great motto and the rule of his life; and the last words uttered to his son in France were these: "My boy, you will one day go back to Santo Domingo; *forget* that *France murdered your father.*" I would call him *Cromwell*, but Cromwell was *only* a *soldier*, and the state he founded *went down* with him into his grave. I would call him *Washington*, but the great Virginian *held slaves*. This man *risked* his *empire* rather than *permit* the slave–trade in the *humblest village* of his dominions.

You think me a fanatic to–night, for you read history, *not* with your *eyes*, but with your *prejudices*. But fifty years hence, when *Truth* gets a hearing, the Muse of History will put *Phocion* for the *Greek*, and *Brutus* for the *Roman*, *Hampden* for *England*, *Lafayette* for *France*, choose *Washington* as the bright, consummate flower of our *earlier* civilization, and *John Brown* the ripe fruit of our *noonday*, then, dipping her pen in the sunlight, will write in the clear blue, above them all, the name of the *soldier*, the *statesman*, the *martyr*, TOUSSAINT L'OUVERTURE.

—WENDELL PHILLIPS, *Toussaint l'Ouverture.*

4. Efficiency Through Change Of Pitch

Speech is simply a modified form of singing: the principal difference being in the fact that in singing the vowel sounds are prolonged and the intervals are short, whereas in speech the words are uttered in what may be called "staccato" tones, the vowels not being specially prolonged and the intervals between the words being more distinct. The fact that in singing we have a larger range of tones does not properly distinguish it from ordinary speech. In speech we have likewise a variation of tones, and even in ordinary conversation there is a difference of from three to six semi–tones, as I have found in my investigations, and in some persons the range is as high as one octave.

—WILLIAM SCHEPPEGRELL, *Popular Science Monthly.*

By pitch, as everyone knows, we mean the relative position of a vocal tone—as, high, medium, low, or any variation between. In public speech we apply it not only to a single utterance, as an exclamation or a monosyllable (*Oh!* or *the*) but to any group of syllables, words, and even sentences that may be spoken in a single tone. This distinction it is important to keep in mind, for the efficient speaker not only changes the pitch of successive syllables (see Chapter VII, "Efficiency through Inflection"), but gives a different pitch to different parts, or word–groups, of successive sentences. It is this phase of the subject which we are considering in this chapter.

Every Change in the Thought Demands a Change in the Voice–Pitch

Whether the speaker follows the rule consciously, unconsciously, or subconsciously, this is the logical basis upon which all good voice variation is made, yet this law is violated more often than any other by *public* speakers. A criminal may disregard a law of the state without detection and punishment, but the speaker who violates this regulation suffers its penalty at once in his loss of effectiveness, while his innocent hearers must endure the monotony—for monotony is not only a sin of the perpetrator, as we have shown, but a plague on the victims as well.

Change of pitch is a stumbling block for almost all beginners, and for many experienced speakers also. This is especially true when the words of the speech have been memorized.

If you wish to hear how pitch–monotony sounds, strike the same note on the piano over and over again. You have in your speaking voice a range of pitch from high to low, with a great many shades between the extremes. With all these notes available there is no excuse for offending the ears and taste of your audience by continually using the one note. True, the reiteration of the same tone in music—as in pedal point on an organ composition—may be made the foundation of beauty, for the harmony weaving about that one basic tone produces a consistent, insistent quality not felt in pure variety of chord sequences. In like manner the intoning voice in a ritual may—though it rarely does—possess a solemn beauty. But the public speaker should shun the monotone as he would a pestilence.

Continual Change of Pitch is Nature's Highest Method

In our search for the principles of efficiency we must continually go back to nature. Listen—really listen—to the birds sing. Which of these feathered tribes are most pleasing in their vocal efforts: those whose voices, though sweet, have little or no range, or those that, like the canary, the lark, and the nightingale, not only possess a considerable range but utter their notes in continual variety of combinations? Even a sweet–toned chirp, when reiterated without change, may grow maddening to the enforced listener.

The little child seldom speaks in a monotonous pitch. Observe the conversations of little folk that you hear on the street or in the home, and note the continual changes of pitch. The unconscious speech of most adults is likewise full of pleasing variations.

Imagine someone speaking the following, and consider if the effect would not be just about as indicated. Remember, we are not now discussing the inflection of single words, but the general pitch in which phrases are spoken.

(High pitch) "I'd like to leave for my vacation tomorrow,—(lower) still, I have so much to do. (Higher) Yet I suppose if I wait until I have time I'll never go."

Repeat this, first in the pitches indicated, and then all in the one pitch, as many speakers would. Observe the difference in naturalness of effect.

The following exercise should be spoken in a purely conversational tone, with numerous changes of pitch. Practise it until your delivery would cause a stranger in the next room to think you were discussing an actual incident with a friend, instead of delivering a memorized monologue. If you are in doubt about the effect you have secured, repeat it to a friend and ask him if it sounds like memorized words. If it does, it is wrong.

A SIMILAR CASE

Jack, I hear you've gone and done it.—Yes, I know; most fellows will; went and tried it once myself, sir, though you see I'm single still. And you met her—did you tell me—down at Newport, last July, and resolved to ask the question at a *soirée*? So did I.

I suppose you left the ball–room, with its music and its light; for they say love's flame is brightest in the darkness of the night. Well, you walked along together, overhead the starlit sky; and I'll bet—old man, confess it—you were frightened. So was I.

So you strolled along the terrace, saw the summer moonlight pour all its radiance on the waters, as they rippled on the shore, till at length you gathered courage, when you saw that none was nigh—did you draw her close and tell her that you loved her? So did I.

Well, I needn't ask you further, and I'm sure I wish you joy. Think I'll wander down and see you when you're married—eh, my boy? When the honeymoon is over and you're settled down, we'll try—What? the deuce you say! Rejected—you rejected? So was I.

—Anonymous.

The necessity for changing pitch is so self–evident that it should be grasped and applied immediately. However, it requires patient drill to free yourself from monotony of pitch.

In natural conversation you think of an idea first, and then find words to express it. In memorized speeches you are liable to speak the words, and then think what they mean—and many speakers seem to trouble very little even about that. Is it any wonder that reversing the process should reverse the result? Get back to nature in your methods of expression.

Read the following selection in a nonchalant manner, never pausing to think what the words really mean. Try it again, carefully studying the thought you have assimilated. Believe the idea, desire to express it effectively, and imagine an audience before you. Look them earnestly in the face and repeat this truth. If you follow directions, you will note that you have made many changes of pitch after several readings.

It is not work that kills men; it is worry. Work is healthy; you can hardly put more upon a man than he can bear. Worry is rust upon the blade. It is not the revolution that destroys the machinery but the friction.

—HENRY WARD BEECHER.

Change of Pitch Produces Emphasis

This is a highly important statement. Variety in pitch maintains the hearer's interest, but one of the surest ways to compel attention—to secure unusual emphasis—is to change the pitch of your voice suddenly and in a marked degree. A great contrast always arouses attention. White shows whiter against black; a cannon roars louder in the Sahara silence than in the Chicago hurly burly—these are simple illustrations of the power of contrast.

"What is Congress going to do next? (High pitch)

I do not know. (Low pitch)

By such sudden change of pitch during a sermon Dr. Newell Dwight Hillis recently achieved great emphasis and suggested the gravity of the question he had raised.

The foregoing order of pitch–change might be reversed with equally good effect, though with a slight change in seriousness—either method produces emphasis when used intelligently, that is, with a common-sense appreciation of the sort of emphasis to be attained.

In attempting these contrasts of pitch it is important to avoid unpleasant extremes. Most speakers pitch their voices too high. One of the secrets of Mr. Bryan's eloquence is his low, bell-like voice. Shakespeare said that a soft, gentle, low voice was "an excellent thing in woman;" it is no less so in man, for a voice need not be blatant to be powerful,—and *must* not be, to be pleasing.

In closing, let us emphasize anew the importance of using variety of pitch. You sing up and down the scale, first touching one note and then another above or below it. Do likewise in speaking.

Thought and individual taste must generally be your guide as to where to use a low, a moderate, or a high pitch.

QUESTIONS AND EXERCISES

1. Name two methods of destroying monotony and gaining force in speaking.

2. Why is a continual change of pitch necessary in speaking?

3. Notice your habitual tones in speaking. Are they too high to be pleasant?

4. Do we express the following thoughts and emotions in a low or a high pitch? Which may be expressed in either high or low pitch? Excitement. Victory. Defeat. Sorrow. Love. Earnestness. Fear.

5. How would you naturally vary the pitch in introducing an explanatory or parenthetical expression like the following:

He started—*that is, he made preparations to start*—on September third.

6. Speak the following lines with as marked variations in pitch as your interpretation of the sense may dictate. Try each line in two different ways. Which, in each instance, is the more effective—and why?

What have I to gain from you? Nothing.

To engage our nation in such a compact would be an infamy.

Note: In the foregoing sentence, experiment as to where the change in pitch would better be made.

Once the flowers distilled their fragrance here, but now see the devastations of war.

He had reckoned without one prime factor—his conscience.

7. Make a diagram of a conversation you have heard, showing where high and low pitches were used. Were these changes in pitch advisable? Why or why not?

8. Read the selections on pages 34, 35, 36, 37 and 38, paying careful attention to the changes in pitch. Reread, substituting low pitch for high, and vice versa.

Selections for Practise

Note: In the following selections, those passages that may best be delivered in a moderate pitch are printed in ordinary (roman) type. Those which may be rendered in a high pitch—do not make the mistake of raising the voice too high—are printed *in italics*. Those which might well be spoken in a low pitch are printed in CAPITALS.

These arrangements, however, are merely suggestive—we cannot make it strong enough that you must use your own judgment in interpreting a selection. Before doing so, however, it is well to practise these passages as they are marked.

Yes, all men labor. RUFUS CHOATE AND DANIEL WEBSTER labor, say the critics. But every man who reads of the labor question knows that it means the movement of the men that earn their living with their hands; *THAT ARE EMPLOYED, AND PAID WAGES: are gathered under roofs of factories, sent out on farms, sent out on ships, gathered on the walls.* In popular acceptation, the working class means the men that work with their hands, for wages, so many hours a day, employed by great capitalists; that work for everybody else. Why do we move for this class? *"Why,"* asks a critic, *"don't you move FOR ALL WORKING-MEN?" BECAUSE, WHILE DANIEL WEBSTER GETS FORTY THOUSAND DOLLARS FOR ARGUING THE MEXICAN CLAIMS, there is no need of* anybody's moving for him. BECAUSE, WHILE RUFUS CHOATE GETS FIVE THOUSAND DOLLARS FOR MAKING ONE ARGUMENT TO A JURY, there is no need of moving for him, or for the men that work with their brains,—that do highly disciplined and skilled labor, invent, and write books. The reason why the Labor movement confines itself to a single class is because that class of work DOES NOT GET PAID, does not get protection. MENTAL LABOR is adequately paid, andMORE THAN ADE-QUATELY protected. IT CAN SHIFT ITS CHANNELS; it can vary according to the supply and demand.

IF A MAN FAILS AS A MINISTER, why, he becomes a railway conductor. IF THAT DOESN'T SUIT HIM, he goes West, and becomes governor of a territory. AND IF HE FINDS HIMSELF INCAPABLE OF EITHER OF THESE POSITIONS, he comes home, and gets to be a city editor. He varies his occupation as he pleases, and doesn't need protection. BUT THE GREAT MASS, CHAINED TO A TRADE, DOOMED TO BE GROUND UP IN THE MILL OF SUPPLY AND DEMAND, THAT WORK SO MANY HOURS A DAY, AND MUST RUN IN THE GREAT RUTS OF BUSINESS,—they are the men whose inadequate protection, whose unfair share of the general product, claims a movement in their behalf.

—WENDELL PHILLIPS.

_KNOWING THE PRICE WE MUST PAY, THE SACRIFICE WE MUST MAKE, THE BURDENS WE MUST CARRY, THE ASSAULTS WE MUST ENDURE— KNOWING FULL WELL THE COST—yet we enlist, and we enlist for the war. FOR WE KNOW THE JUSTICE OF OUR CAUSE, and we know, too, its certain triumph.

NOT RELUCTANTLY THEN, but eagerly, not with faint hearts BUT STRONG, do we now advance upon the enemies of the people. FOR THE CALL THAT COMES TO US is the call that came to our fathers_.

As they responded so shall we.

"_HE HATH SOUNDED FORTH A TRUMPET that shall never call retreat. HE IS SIFTING OUT THE HEARTS OF MEN before His judgment seat. OH, BE SWIFT OUR SOULS TO ANSWER HIM, BE JUBILANT OUR FEET, Our God is marching on_."

—ALBERT J. BEVERIDGE.

Remember that two sentences, or two parts of the same sentence, which contain changes of thought, cannot possibly be given effectively in the same key. Let us repeat, every big change of thought requires a big change of pitch. What the beginning student will think are big changes of pitch will be monotonously alike. Learn to speak some thoughts in a very high tone—others in a *very, very* low tone. *DEVELOP RANGE.* It is almost impossible to use too much of it.

HAPPY AM I THAT THIS MISSION HAS BROUGHT MY FEET AT LAST TO PRESS NEW ENGLAND'S HISTORIC SOIL and my eyes to the knowledge of her beauty and her thrift. Here within touch of Plymouth Rock and Bunker Hill—*WHERE WEBSTER THUNDERED and Longfellow sang, Emerson thought AND CHANNING PREACHED—HERE IN THE CRADLE OF AMERICAN LETTERS and almost of American liberty,* I hasten to make the obeisance that every American owes New England when first he stands uncovered in her mighty presence. *Strange apparition!* This stern and unique figure—carved from the ocean and the wilderness—its majesty kindling and growing amid the storms of winter and of wars—until at last the gloom was broken, *ITS BEAUTY DISCLOSED IN THE SUNSHINE, and the heroic workers rested at its base*—while startled kings and emperors gazed and marveled that from the rude touch of this handful cast on a bleak and unknown shore should have come the *embodied genius of human government AND THE PERFECTED MODEL OF HUMAN LIBERTY!* God bless the memory of those immortal workers, and prosper the fortunes of their living sons—and perpetuate the inspiration of their handiwork....

Far to the South, Mr. President, separated from this section by a line—*once defined in irrepressible difference, once traced in fratricidal blood, AND NOW, THANK GOD, BUT A VANISHING SHADOW—lies the fairest and richest domain of this earth. It is the home of a brave and hospitable people. THERE IS CENTERED ALL THAT CAN PLEASE OR PROSPER HUMANKIND. A PERFECT CLIMATE ABOVE a fertile soil* yields to the husbandman every product of the temperate zone.

There, by night *the cotton whitens beneath the stars,* and by day *THE WHEAT LOCKS THE SUNSHINE IN ITS BEARDED SHEAF.* In the same field the clover steals the fragrance of the wind, and tobacco catches the quick aroma of the rains. *THERE ARE MOUNTAINS STORED WITH EXHAUSTLESS TREASURES: forests—vast and primeval;* and rivers that, *tumbling or loitering, run wanton to the sea.* Of the three essential items of all industries—cotton, iron and wood—that region has easy control. *IN COTTON, a fixed monopoly—IN IRON, proven supremacy—IN TIMBER, the reserve supply of the Republic.* From this assured and permanent advantage, against which artificial conditions cannot much longer prevail, has grown an amazing system of industries. Not maintained by human contrivance of tariff or capital, afar off from the fullest and cheapest source of supply, but resting in divine assurance, within touch of field and mine and forest—not set amid costly farms from which competition has driven the farmer in despair, but amid cheap and sunny lands, rich with agriculture, to which neither season nor soil has set a limit—this system of industries is mounting to a splendor that shall dazzle and illumine the world. *THAT, SIR, is the picture and the promise of my home—A LAND BETTER AND FAIRER THAN I HAVE TOLD YOU, and yet but fit setting in its material excellence for the loyal and gentle quality of its citizenship.*

This hour little needs the *LOYALTY THAT IS LOYAL TO ONE SECTION and yet holds the other in enduring suspicion and estrangement.* Give us the *broad* and *perfect loyalty that loves and trusts GEORGIA* alike with *Massachusetts*—that knows no *SOUTH*, no *North*, no *EAST*, no *West*, but *endears with equal and patriotic love* every foot of our soil, every State of our Union.

A MIGHTY DUTY, SIR, AND A MIGHTY INSPIRATION impels every one of us to–night to lose in patriotic consecration WHATEVER ESTRANGES, WHATEVER DIVIDES.

WE, SIR, are Americans—AND WE STAND FOR HUMAN LIBERTY! The uplifting force of the American idea is under every throne on earth. *France, Brazil—THESE ARE OUR VICTORIES. To redeem the earth from kingcraft and oppression—THIS IS OUR MISSION! AND WE SHALL NOT FAIL.* God has sown in our soil the seed of His millennial harvest, and He will not lay the sickle to the ripening crop until His full and perfect day has come. *OUR HISTORY, SIR, has been a constant and expanding miracle, FROM PLYMOUTH ROCK AND JAMESTOWN, all the* way—aye, even from the hour when from the voiceless and traceless ocean a new world rose to the sight of the inspired sailor. As we approach the fourth centennial of that stupendous day—when the old world will come to *marvel* and to *learn* amid our gathered treasures— let us resolve to crown the miracles of our past with the spectacle of a Republic, *compact, united INDISSOLUBLE IN THE BONDS OF LOVE—*

loving from the Lakes to the Gulf—the wounds of war healed in every heart as on every hill, *serene and resplendent AT THE SUMMIT OF HU-MAN ACHIEVEMENT AND EARTHLY GLORY, blazing out the path and making clear the way up which all the nations of the earth, must come in God's appointed time!*

—HENRY W. GRADY, *The Race Problem.*

... I WOULD CALL HIM NAPOLEON, but Napoleon made his way to empire *over broken oaths and through a sea of blood.* This man never broke his word. "No Retaliation" was his great motto and the rule of his life; *AND THE LAST WORDS UTTERED TO HIS SON IN FRANCE WERE THESE: "My boy, you will one day go back to Santo Domingo; forget that France murdered your father." I WOULD CALL HIM CROMWELL,* but Cromwell *was only a soldier, and the state he founded went down with him into his grave. I WOULD CALL HIM WASHINGTON,* but the great Virginian *held slaves. THIS MAN RISKED HIS EMPIRE rather than permit the slave–trade in the humblest village of his dominions.*

YOU THINK ME A FANATIC TO–NIGHT, for you read history, *not with your eyes, BUT WITH YOUR PREJUDICES.* But fifty years hence, when Truth gets a hearing, the Muse of History will put *PHOCION for the Greek,* and *BRUTUS for the Roman, HAMPDEN for England, LAFAYETTE for France,* choose *WASHINGTON as the bright, consummate flower of our EARLIER civilization, AND JOHN BROWN the ripe fruit of our NOONDAY,* then, dipping her pen in the sunlight, will write in the clear blue, above them all, the name of *THE SOLDIER, THE STATESMAN, THE MARTYR, TOUSSAINT L'OUVERTURE.*

—Wendell Phillips, *Toussaint l'Ouverture.*

Drill on the following selections for change of pitch: Beecher's "Abraham Lincoln," p. 76; Seward's "Irrepressible Conflict," p. 67; Everett's "History of Liberty," p. 78; Grady's "The Race Problem," p. 36; and Beveridge's "Pass Prosperity Around," p. 470.

5. Efficiency Through Change Of Pace

Hear how he clears the points o' Faith
Wi' rattlin' an' thumpin'!
Now meekly calm, now wild in wrath,
He's stampin' an' he's jumpin'.

—ROBERT BURNS, *Holy Fair.*

The Latins have bequeathed to us a word that has no precise equivalent in our tongue, therefore we have accepted it, body unchanged—it is the word *tempo*, and means *rate of movement*, as measured by the time consumed in executing that movement.

Thus far its use has been largely limited to the vocal and musical arts, but it would not be surprising to hear tempo applied to more concrete matters, for it perfectly illustrates the real meaning of the word to say that an ox–cart moves in slow tempo, an express train in a fast tempo. Our guns that fire six hundred times a minute, shoot at a fast tempo; the old muzzle loader that required three minutes to load, shot at a slow tempo. Every musician understands this principle: it requires longer to sing a half note than it does an eighth note.

Now tempo is a tremendously important element in good platform work, for when a speaker delivers a whole address at very nearly the same rate of speed he is depriving himself of one of his chief means of emphasis and power. The baseball pitcher, the bowler in cricket, the tennis server, all know the value of change of pace—change of tempo—in delivering their ball, and so must the public speaker observe its power.

Change of Tempo Lends Naturalness to the Delivery

Naturalness, or at least seeming naturalness, as was explained in the chapter on "Monotony," is greatly to be desired, and a continual change of tempo will go a long way towards establishing it. Mr. Howard Lindsay, Stage Manager for Miss Margaret Anglin, recently said to the present writer that change of pace was one of the most effective tools of the actor. While it must be admitted that the stilted mouthings of many actors indicate cloudy mirrors, still the public speaker would do well to study the actor's use of tempo.

There is, however, a more fundamental and effective source at which to study naturalness—a trait which, once lost, is shy of recapture: that source is the common conversation of any well–bred circle. *This* is the standard we strive to reach on both stage and platform—with certain differences, of course, which will appear as we go on. If speaker and actor were to reproduce with absolute fidelity every variation of utterance—every whisper, grunt, pause, silence, and explosion— of conversation as we find it typically in everyday life, much of the interest would leave the public utterance. Naturalness in public address is something more than faithful reproduction of nature—it is the reproduction of those *typical* parts of nature's work which are truly representative of the whole.

The realistic story–writer understands this in writing dialogue, and we must take it into account in seeking for naturalness through change of tempo.

Suppose you speak the first of the following sentences in a slow tempo, the second quickly, observing how natural is the effect. Then speak both with the same rapidity and note the difference.

I can't recall what I did with my knife. Oh, now I remember I gave it to Mary.

We see here that a change of tempo often occurs in the same sentence—for tempo applies not only to single words, groups of words, and groups of sentences, but to the major parts of a public speech as well.

QUESTIONS AND EXERCISES

1. In the following, speak the words "long, long while" very slowly; the rest of the sentence is spoken in moderately rapid tempo.

When you and I behind the Veil are past,
Oh but the long, long while the world shall last,
Which of our coming and departure heeds,
As the seven seas should heed a pebble cast.

Note: In the following selections the passages that should be given a fast tempo are in italics; those that should be given in a slow tempo are in small capitals. Practise these selections, and then try others, changing from fast to slow tempo on different parts, carefully noting the effect.

2. No MIRABEAU, NAPOLEON, BURNS, CROMWELL, NO *man* ADEQUATE *to* DO ANYTHING *but is first of all in* RIGHT EARNEST *about it—what I call* A SINCERE *man. I should say* SINCERI-TY, *a* GREAT, DEEP, GENUINE SINCERITY, *is the first* CHARACTERISTIC *of a man in any way* HEROIC. *Not the sincerity that* CALLS *itself sincere. Ah no. That is a very poor matter indeed—*A SHALLOW, BRAGGART, CON-SCIOUS *sincerity, oftenest* SELF–CONCEIT *mainly. The* GREAT MAN'S SINCERITY *is of a kind he* CANNOT SPEAK OF. *Is* NOT CONSCIOUS *of.—*THOMAS CARLYLE.

3. TRUE WORTH *is in* BEING—NOT SEEMING—*in doing each day that goes by* SOME LITTLE GOOD, *not in* DREAMING *of* GREAT THINGS *to do by and by. For whatever men say in their* BLINDNESS, *and in spite of the* FOLLIES *of* YOUTH, *there is nothing so* KINGLY *as* KINDNESS, *and nothing so* ROYAL *as* TRUTH.—*Anonymous.*

4. To get a natural effect, where would you use slow and where fast tempo in the following?

FOOL'S GOLD

See him there, cold and gray,
Watch him as he tries to play;
No, he doesn't know the way—
He began to learn too late.
She's a grim old hag, is Fate,
For she let him have his pile,
Smiling to herself the while,
Knowing what the cost would be,
When he'd found the Golden Key.
Multimillionaire is he,
Many times more rich than we;
But at that I wouldn't trade
With the bargain that he made.
Came here many years ago,

Not a person did he know;
Had the money–hunger bad—
Mad for money, piggish mad;
Didn't let a joy divert him,
Didn't let a sorrow hurt him,
Let his friends and kin desert him,
While he planned and plugged and hurried

On his quest for gold and power.
Every single wakeful hour
With a money thought he'd dower;
All the while as he grew older,
And grew bolder, he grew colder.
And he thought that some day
He would take the time to play;
But, say—he was wrong.
Life's a song;
In the spring
Youth can sing and can fling;
But joys wing
When we're older,
Like birds when it's colder.
The roses were red as he went rushing by,
And glorious tapestries hung in the sky,
And the clover was waving
'Neath honey–bees' slaving;
A bird over there
Rounde layed a soft air;
But the man couldn't spare
Time for gathering flowers,
Or resting in bowers,
Or gazing at skies
That gladdened the eyes.
So he kept on and swept on
Through mean, sordid years.
Now he's up to his ears
In the choicest of stocks.
He owns endless blocks
Of houses and shops,
And the stream never stops

Pouring into his banks.
I suppose that he ranks
Pretty near to the top.
What I have wouldn't sop
His ambition one tittle;
And yet with my little
I don't care to trade

With the bargain he made.
Just watch him to–day—
See him trying to play.
He's come back for blue skies.
But they're in a new guise—
Winter's here, all is gray,
The birds are away,
The meadows are brown,
The leaves lie aground,
And the gay brook that wound
With a swirling and whirling
Of waters, is furling
Its bosom in ice.
And he hasn't the price,
With all of his gold,
To buy what he sold.
He knows now the cost
Of the spring–time he lost,
Of the flowers he tossed
From his way,
And, say,
He'd pay
Any price if the day
Could be made not so gray.
He can't play.

—HERBERT KAUFMAN. Used by permission of *Everybody's Magazine.*

Change of Tempo Prevents Monotony

The canary in the cage before the window is adding to the beauty and charm of his singing by a continual change of tempo. If King Solomon had been an orator he undoubtedly would have gathered wisdom from the song of the wild birds as well as from the bees. Imagine a song written with but quarter notes. Imagine an auto with only one speed.

EXERCISES

1. Note the change of tempo indicated in the following, and how it gives a pleasing variety. Read it aloud. (Fast tempo is indicated by italics, slow by small capitals.)

And he thought that some day he would take the time to play; but, say— HE WAS WRONG. LIFE'S A SONG; *in the* SPRING YOUTH *can* SING *and can* FLING; BUT JOYS WING WHEN WE'RE OLDER, LIKE THE BIRDS *when it's* COLDER. *The roses were red as he went rushing by, and glorious tapestries hung in the sky.*

2. Turn to "Fools Gold," on Page 42, and deliver it in an unvaried tempo: note how monotonous is the result. This poem requires a great many changes of tempo, and is an excellent one for practise.

3. Use the changes of tempo indicated in the following, noting how they prevent monotony. Where no change of tempo is indicated, use a moderate speed. Too much of variety would really be a return to monotony.

THE MOB

"A MOB KILLS THE WRONG MAN" *was flashed in a newspaper headline lately. The mob is an* IRRESPONSIBLE, UNTHINKING MASS. *It always destroys* BUT NEVER CONSTRUCTS. *It criticises* BUT NEVER CREATES.

Utter a great truth AND THE MOB WILL HATE YOU. *See how it condemned* DANTE *to* EXILE. *Encounter the dangers of the unknown world for its benefit,* AND THE MOB WILL DECLARE YOU CRAZY. *It ridiculed* COLUMBUS, *and for discovering a new world* GAVE HIM PRISON AND CHAINS.

Write a poem to thrill human hearts with pleasure, AND THE MOB WILL ALLOW YOU TO GO HUNGRY: THE BLIND HOMER BEGGED BREAD THROUGH THE STREETS. *Invent a machine to save labor* AND THE MOB WILL DECLARE YOU ITS ENEMY. *Less than a hundred years ago a furious rabble smashed Thimonier's invention, the sewing machine.*

BUILD A STEAMSHIP TO CARRY MERCHANDISE AND ACCELERATE TRAVEL *and the mob will call you a fool.* A MOB LINED THE SHORES OF THE HUDSON RIVER TO LAUGH AT THE MAIDEN ATTEMPT OF "FULTON'S FOLLY," *as they called his little steamboat.*

Emerson says: "A mob is a society of bodies voluntarily bereaving themselves of reason and traversing its work. The mob is man voluntarily descended to the nature of the beast. *Its fit hour of activity* is NIGHT. ITS ACTIONS ARE INSANE, *like its whole constitution. It persecutes a principle*—IT WOULD WHIP A RIGHT. It would tar and feather justice by inflicting fire and outrage upon the house and persons of those who have these."

The mob spirit stalks abroad in our land today. Every week gives a fresh victim to its malignant cry for blood. There were 48 persons killed by mobs in the United States in 1913; 64 in 1912, and 71 in 1911. Among the 48 last year were a woman and a child. Two victims were proven innocent after their death.

IN 399 B.C. A DEMAGOG APPEALED TO THE POPULAR MOB TO HAVE SOCRATES PUT TO DEATH *and he was sentenced to the hemlock cup.* FOURTEEN HUNDRED YEARS AFTERWARD AN ENTHUSIAST APPEALED TO THE POPULAR MOB *and all Europe plunged into the Holy Land to kill and mangle the heathen. In the seventeenth century a demagog appealed to the ignorance of men* AND TWENTY PEOPLE WERE EXECUTED AT SALEM, MASS., WITHIN SIX MONTHS FOR WITCHCRAFT. *Two thousand years ago the mob yelled, "RELEASE UNTO US BARABBAS"*—AND BARABBAS WAS A MURDERER!

—From an Editorial by D.C. in "Leslie's Weekly," by permission.

Present–day business is as unlike OLD–TIME BUSINESS as the OLD–TIME OX–CART is unlike the *present–day locomotive.* INVENTION has made the *whole world over again. The railroad, telegraph, telephone* have bound the people of MODERN NATIONS into FAMILIES. *To do the business of these closely knit millions in every modern country* GREAT BUSINESS CONCERNS CAME INTO BEING. *What we call big business is the* CHILD OF THE ECONOMIC PROGRESS OF MANKIND. *So warfare to destroy big business* is FOOLISH BECAUSE IT CAN NOT SUCCEED *and wicked* BECAUSE IT OUGHT NOT TO SUCCEED. *Warfare to destroy big business does not hurt big business, which always comes out on top,* SO

MUCH AS IT HURTS ALL OTHER BUSINESS WHICH, IN SUCH A WAR-FARE, NEVER COME OUT ON TOP.

—A.J. BEVERIDGE.

Change of Tempo Produces Emphasis

Any big change of tempo is emphatic and will catch the attention. You may scarcely be conscious that a passenger train is moving when it is flying over the rails at ninety miles an hour, but if it slows down very suddenly to a ten–mile gait your attention will be drawn to it very decidedly. You may forget that you are listening to music as you dine, but let the orchestra either increase or diminish its tempo in a very marked degree and your attention will be arrested at once.

This same principle will procure emphasis in a speech. If you have a point that you want to bring home to your audience forcefully, make a sudden and great change of tempo, and they will be powerless to keep from paying attention to that point. Recently the present writer saw a play in which these lines were spoken:

"I don't want you to forget what I said. I want you to remember it the longest day you—I don't care if you've got six guns." The part up to the dash was delivered in a very slow tempo, the remainder was named out at lightning speed, as the character who was spoken to drew a revolver. The effect was so emphatic that the lines are remembered six months afterwards, while most of the play has faded from memory. The student who has powers of observation will see this principle applied by all our best actors in their efforts to get emphasis where emphasis is due. But remember that the emotion in the matter must warrant the intensity in the manner, or the effect will be ridiculous. Too many public speakers are impressive over nothing.

Thought rather than rules must govern you while practising change of pace. It is often a matter of no consequence which part of a sentence is spoken slowly and which is given in fast tempo. The main thing to be desired is the change itself. For example, in the selection, "The Mob," on page 46, note the last paragraph. Reverse the instructions given, delivering everything that is marked for slow tempo, quickly; and everything that is marked for quick tempo, slowly. You will note that the force or meaning of the passage has not been destroyed.

However, many passages cannot be changed to a slow tempo without destroying their force. Instances: The Patrick Henry speech on page 110, and the following passage from Whittier's "Barefoot Boy."

O for boyhood's time of June, crowding years in one brief moon, when all things I heard or saw, me, their master, waited for. I was rich in flowers and trees, humming–birds and honey–bees; for my sport the squirrel played; plied the snouted mole his spade; for my taste the blackberry cone purpled over hedge and stone; laughed the brook for my delight through the day and through the night, whispering at the garden wall, talked with me from fall to fall; mine the sand–rimmed pickerel pond; mine the walnut slopes beyond; mine, an bending orchard trees, apples of Hesperides! Still, as my horizon grew, larger grew my riches, too; all the world I saw or knew seemed a complex Chinese toy, fashioned for a barefoot boy!

—J.G. WHITTIER.

Be careful in regulating your tempo not to get your movement too fast. This is a common fault with amateur speakers. Mrs. Siddons rule was, "Take time." A hundred years ago there was used in medical circles a preparation known as "the shot gun remedy;" it was a mixture of about fifty different ingredients, and was given to the patient in the hope that at least one of them would prove efficacious! That seems a rather poor scheme for medical practice, but it is good to use "shot gun" tempo for most speeches, as it gives a variety. Tempo, like diet, is best when mixed.

QUESTIONS AND EXERCISES

1. Define tempo.

2. What words come from the same root?

3. What is meant by a change of tempo?

4. What effects are gained by it?

5. Name three methods of destroying monotony and gaining force in speaking.

6. Note the changes of tempo in a conversation or speech that you

hear. Were they well made? Why? Illustrate.

7. Read selections on pages 34, 35, 36, 37, and 38, paying careful attention to change of tempo.

8. As a rule, excitement, joy, or intense anger take a fast tempo, while sorrow, and sentiments of great dignity or solemnity tend to a slow tempo. Try to deliver Lincoln's Gettysburg speech (page 50), in a fast tempo, or Patrick Henry's speech (page 110), in a slow tempo, and note how ridiculous the effect will be.

Practise the following selections, noting carefully where the tempo may be changed to advantage. Experiment, making numerous changes. Which one do you like best?

DEDICATION OF GETTYSBURG CEMETERY

Fourscore and seven years ago, our fathers brought forth upon this continent a new nation, conceived in liberty and dedicated to the proposition that all men are created equal. Now we are engaged in a great civil war, testing whether that nation—or any nation so conceived and so dedicated—can long endure.

We are met on a great battlefield of that war. We are met to dedicate a portion of it as the final resting–place of those who have given their lives that that nation might live. It is altogether fitting and proper that we should do this.

But, in a larger sense, we cannot dedicate, we cannot consecrate, we cannot hallow, this ground. The brave men, living and dead, who struggled here, have consecrated it, far above our power to add or to detract. The world will very little note nor long remember what we say here; but it can never forget what they did here.

It is for us, the living, rather, to be dedicated here to the unfinished work they have thus far so nobly carried on. It is rather for us to be here dedicated to the great task remaining before us: that from these honored dead we take increased devotion to that cause for which they here gave the last full measure of devotion; that we here highly resolve that these dead shall not have died in vain; that the nation shall, under God, have a new birth of freedom, and that government of the people, by the people, for the people, shall not perish from the earth.

—ABRAHAM LINCOLN.

A PLEA FOR CUBA

[This deliberative oration was delivered by Senator Thurston in the United States Senate on March 24, 1898. It is recorded in full in the *Congressional Record* of that date. Mrs. Thurston died in Cuba. As a dying request she urged her husband, who was investigating affairs in the island, to do his utmost to induce the United States to intervene— hence this oration.]

Mr. President, I am here by command of silent lips to speak once and for all upon the Cuban situation. I shall endeavor to be honest, conservative, and just. I have no purpose to stir the public passion to any action not necessary and imperative to meet the duties and necessities of American responsibility, Christian humanity, and national honor. I would shirk this task if I could, but I dare not. I cannot satisfy my conscience except by speaking, and speaking now.

I went to Cuba firmly believing that the condition of affairs there had been greatly exaggerated by the press, and my own efforts were directed in the first instance to the attempted exposure of these supposed exaggerations. There has undoubtedly been much sensationalism in the journalism of the time, but as to the condition of affairs in Cuba, there has been no exaggeration, because exaggeration has been impossible.

Under the inhuman policy of Weyler not less than four hundred thousand self–supporting, simple, peaceable, defenseless country people were driven from their homes in the agricultural portions of the Spanish provinces to the cities, and imprisoned upon the barren waste outside the residence portions of these cities and within the lines of intrenchment established a little way beyond. Their humble homes were burned, their fields laid waste, their implements of husbandry destroyed, their live stock and food supplies for the most part confiscated. Most of the people were old men, women, and children. They were thus placed in hopeless imprisonment, without shelter or food. There was no work for them in the cities to which they were driven. They were left with nothing to depend upon except the scanty charity of the inhabitants of the cities and with slow starvation their inevitable fate....

The pictures in the American newspapers of the starving reconcentrados are true. They can all be duplicated by the thousands. I never before saw, and please God I may never again see, so deplorable a sight as the reconcentrados in the suburbs of Matanzas. I can never forget to my dying day the hopeless anguish in their despairing eyes. Huddled about their little bark huts, they raised no voice of appeal to us for alms as we went among them....

Men, women, and children stand silent, famishing with hunger. Their only appeal comes from their sad eyes, through which one looks as through an open window into their agonizing souls.

The government of Spain has not appropriated and will not appropriate one dollar to save these people. They are now being attended and nursed and administered to by the charity of the United States. Think of the spectacle! We are feeding these citizens of Spain; we are nursing their sick; we are saving such as can be saved, and yet there are those who still say it is right for us to send food, but we must keep hands off. I say that the time has come when muskets ought to go with the food.

We asked the governor if he knew of any relief for these people except through the charity of the United States. He did not. We asked him, "When do you think the time will come that these people can be placed in a position of self–support?" He replied to us, with deep feeling, "Only the good God or the great government of the United States will answer that question." I hope and believe that the good God by the great government of the United States will answer that question.

I shall refer to these horrible things no further. They are there. God pity me, I have seen them; they will remain in my mind forever—and this is almost the twentieth century. Christ died nineteen hundred years ago, and Spain is a Christian nation. She has set up more crosses in more lands, beneath more skies, and under them has butchered more people than all the other nations of the earth combined. Europe may tolerate her existence as long as the people of the Old World wish. God grant that before another Christmas morning the last vestige of Spanish tyranny and oppression will have vanished from the Western Hemisphere!...

The time for action has come. No greater reason for it can exist to–morrow than exists to–day. Every hour's delay only adds another chapter to the awful story of misery and death. Only one power can intervene—the United States of America. Ours is the one great nation in the world, the mother of American republics. She holds a position of trust and responsibility toward the peoples and affairs of the whole Western Hemisphere. It was her glorious example which inspired the patriots of Cuba to raise the flag of liberty in her eternal hills. We cannot refuse to accept this responsibility which the God of the universe has placed upon us as the one great power in the New World. We must act! What shall our action be?

Against the intervention of the United States in this holy cause there is but one voice of dissent; that voice is the voice of the money–changers. They fear war! Not because of any Christian or ennobling sentiment against war and in favor of peace, but because they fear that a declaration of war, or the intervention which might result in war, would have a depressing effect upon the stock market. Let them go. They do not represent American sentiment; they do not represent American patriotism. Let them take their chances as they can. Their weal or woe is of but little importance to the liberty–loving people of the United States. They will not do the fighting; their blood will not flow; they will keep on dealing in options on human life. Let the men whose loyalty is to the dollar stand aside while the men whose loyalty is to the flag come to the front.

Mr. President, there is only one action possible, if any is taken; that is, intervention for the independence of the island. But we cannot intervene and save Cuba without the exercise of force, and force means war; war means blood. The lowly Nazarene on the shores of Galilee preached the divine doctrine of love, "Peace on earth, good will toward men." Not peace on earth at the expense of liberty and humanity. Not good will toward men who despoil, enslave, degrade, and starve to death their fellow–men. I believe in the doctrine of Christ. I believe in the doctrine of peace; but, Mr. President, men must have liberty before there can come abiding peace.

Intervention means force. Force means war. War means blood. But it will be God's force. When has a battle for humanity and liberty ever been won except by force? What barricade of wrong, injustice, and oppression has ever been carried except by force?

Force compelled the signature of unwilling royalty to the great Magna Charta; force put life into the Declaration of Independence and made effective the Emancipation Proclamation; force beat with naked hands upon the iron gateway of the Bastile and made reprisal in one awful hour for centuries of kingly crime; force waved the flag of revolution over Bunker Hill and marked the snows of Valley Forge with blood–stained feet; force held the broken line of Shiloh, climbed the flame–swept hill at Chattanooga, and stormed the clouds on Lookout Heights; force marched with Sherman to the sea, rode with Sheridan in the valley of the Shenandoah, and gave Grant victory at Appomattox; force saved the Union, kept the stars in the flag, made "niggers" men. The time for God's force has come again. Let the impassioned lips of American patriots once more take up the song:—

"In the beauty of the lilies, Christ was born across the sea. With a glory in His bosom that transfigures you and me; As He died to make men holy, let us die to make men free. While God is marching on."

Others may hesitate, others may procrastinate, others may plead for further diplomatic negotiation, which means delay; but for me, I am ready to act now, and for my action I am ready to answer to my conscience, my country, and my God.

—JAMES MELLEN THURSTON.

6. Pause And Power

The true business of the literary artist is to plait or weave his meaning, involving it around itself; so that each sentence, by successive phrases, shall first come into a kind of knot, and then, after a moment of suspended meaning, solve and clear itself.

—GEORGE SAINTSBURY, on *English Prose Style*, in 'Miscellaneous Essays'.

... pause ... has a distinctive value, expressed in silence; in other words, while the voice is waiting, the music of the movement is going on ... To manage it, with its delicacies and compensations, requires that same fineness of ear on which we must depend for all faultless prose rhythm. When there is no compensation, when the pause is inadvertent ... there is a sense of jolting and lack, as if some pin or fastening had fallen out.

—JOHN FRANKLIN GENUNG, *The Working Principles of Rhetoric*.

Pause, in public speech, is not mere silence—it is silence made designedly eloquent.

When a man says: "I–uh–it is with profound–ah–pleasure that–er–I have been permitted to speak to you tonight and–uh–uh–I should say–er"—that is not pausing; that is stumbling. It is conceivable that a speaker may be effective in spite of stumbling—but never because of it.

On the other hand, one of the most important means of developing power in public speaking is to pause either before or after, or both before and after, an important word or phrase. No one who would be a forceful speaker can afford to neglect this principle—one of the most significant that has ever been inferred from listening to great orators. Study this potential device until you have absorbed and assimilated it.

It would seem that this principle of rhetorical pause ought to be easily grasped and applied, but a long experience in training both college men and maturer speakers has demonstrated that the device is no more readily understood by the average man when it is first explained to him than if it were spoken in Hindoostani. Perhaps this is because we do not eagerly devour the fruit of experience when it is impressively set before us on the platter of authority; we like to pluck fruit for ourselves—it not only tastes better, but we never forget that tree! Fortunately, this is no difficult task, in this instance, for the trees stand thick all about us.

One man is pleading the cause of another:

"This man, my friends, has made this wonderful sacrifice—for you and me."

Did not the pause surprisingly enhance the power of this statement? See how he gathered up reserve force and impressiveness to deliver the words "for you and me." Repeat this passage without making a pause. Did it lose in effectiveness?

Naturally enough, during a premeditated pause of this kind the mind of the speaker is concentrated on the thought to which he is about to give expression. He will not dare to allow his thoughts to wander for an instant—he will rather supremely center his thought and his emotion upon the sacrifice whose service, sweetness and divinity he is enforcing by his appeal.

Concentration, then, is the big word here—no pause without it can perfectly hit the mark.

Efficient pausing accomplishes one or all of four results:

1. Pause Enables the Mind of the Speaker to Gather His Forces Before Delivering the Final Volley

It is often dangerous to rush into battle without pausing for preparation or waiting for recruits. Consider Custer's massacre as an instance.

You can light a match by holding it beneath a lens and concentrating the sun's rays. You would not expect the match to flame if you jerked the lens back and forth quickly. Pause, and the lens gathers the heat. Your thoughts will not set fire to the minds of your hearers unless you pause to gather the force that comes by a second or two of concentration. Maple trees and gas wells are rarely tapped continually; when a stronger flow is wanted, a pause is made, nature has time to gather her reserve forces, and when the tree or the well is reopened, a stronger flow is the result.

Use the same common sense with your mind. If you would make a thought particularly effective, pause just before its utterance, concentrate your mind–energies, and then give it expression with renewed vigor. Carlyle was right: "Speak not, I passionately entreat thee, till thy thought has silently matured itself. Out of silence comes thy strength. Speech is silvern, Silence is golden; Speech is human, Silence is divine."

Silence has been called the father of speech. It should be. Too many of our public speeches have no fathers. They ramble along without pause or break. Like Tennyson's brook, they run on forever. Listen to little children, the policeman on the corner, the family conversation around the table, and see how many pauses they naturally use, for they are unconscious of effects. When we get before an audience, we throw most of our natural methods of expression to the wind, and strive after artificial effects. Get back to the methods of nature—and pause.

2. Pause Prepares the Mind of the Auditor to Receive Your Message

Herbert Spencer said that all the universe is in motion. So it is—and all perfect motion is rhythm. Part of rhythm is rest. Rest follows activity all through nature. Instances: day and night; spring—summer—autumn—winter; a period of rest between breaths; an instant of complete rest between heart beats. Pause, and give the attention–powers of your audience a rest. What you say after such a silence will then have a great deal more effect.

When your country cousins come to town, the noise of a passing car will awaken them, though it seldom affects a seasoned city dweller. By the continual passing of cars his attention–power has become deadened. In one who visits the city but seldom, attention–value is insistent. To him the noise comes after a long pause; hence its power. To you, dweller in the city, there is no pause; hence the low attention–value. After riding on a train several hours you will become so accustomed to its roar that it will lose its attention–value, unless the train should stop for a while and start again. If you attempt to listen to a clock–tick that is so far away that you can barely hear it, you will find that at times you are unable to distinguish it, but in a few moments the sound becomes distinct again. Your mind will pause for rest whether you desire it to do so or not.

The attention of your audience will act in quite the same way. Recognize this law and prepare for it—by pausing. Let it be repeated: the thought that follows a pause is much more dynamic than if no pause had occurred. What is said to you of a night will not have the same effect on your mind as if it had been uttered in the morning when your attention had been lately refreshed by the pause of sleep. We are told on the first page of the Bible that even the Creative Energy of God rested on the "seventh day." You may be sure, then, that the frail finite mind of your audience will likewise demand rest. Observe nature, study her laws, and obey them in your speaking.

3. Pause Creates Effective Suspense

Suspense is responsible for a great share of our interest in life; it will be the same with your speech. A play or a novel is often robbed of much of its interest if you know the plot beforehand. We like to keep guessing as to the outcome. The ability to create suspense is part of woman's power to hold the other sex. The circus acrobat employs this principle when he fails purposely in several attempts to perform a feat, and then achieves it. Even the deliberate manner in which he arranges the preliminaries increases our expectation—we like to be kept waiting. In the last act of the play, "Polly of the Circus," there is a circus scene in which a little dog turns a backward somersault on the back of a running pony. One night when he hesitated and had to be coaxed and worked with a long time before he would perform his feat he got a great deal more applause than when he did his trick at once. We not only like to wait but we appreciate what we wait for. If fish bite too readily the sport soon ceases to be a sport.

It is this same principle of suspense that holds you in a Sherlock Holmes story—you wait to see how the mystery is solved, and if it is solved too soon you throw down the tale unfinished. Wilkie Collins' receipt for fiction writing well applies to public speech: "Make 'em laugh; make 'em weep; make 'em wait." Above all else make them wait; if they will not do that you may be sure they will neither laugh nor weep.

Thus pause is a valuable instrument in the hands of a trained speaker to arouse and maintain suspense. We once heard Mr. Bryan say in a speech: "It was my privilege to hear"—and he paused, while the audience wondered for a second whom it was his privilege to hear - "the great evangelist"—and he paused again; we knew a little more about the man he had heard, but still wondered to which evangelist he referred; and then he concluded: "Dwight L. Moody." Mr. Bryan paused slightly again and continued: "I came to regard him"—here he paused again and held the audience in a brief moment of suspense as to how he had regarded Mr. Moody, then continued - "as the greatest preacher of his day." Let the dashes illustrate pauses and we have the following:

"It was my privilege to hear—the great evangelist—Dwight L. Moody.—I came to regard him—as the greatest preacher of his day."

The unskilled speaker would have rattled this off with neither pause nor suspense, and the sentences would have fallen flat upon the audience. It is precisely the application of these small things that makes much of the difference between the successful and the unsuccessful speaker.

4. Pausing After An Important Idea Gives it Time to Penetrate

Any Missouri farmer will tell you that a rain that falls too fast will run off into the creeks and do the crops but little good. A story is told of a country deacon praying for rain in this manner: "Lord, don't send us any chunk floater. Just give us a good old drizzle–drazzle." A speech, like a rain, will not do anybody much good if it comes too fast to soak in. The farmer's wife follows this same principle in doing her washing when she puts the clothes in water—and pauses for several hours that the water may soak in. The physician puts cocaine on your turbinates—and pauses to let it take hold before he removes them. Why do we use this principle everywhere except in the communication of ideas? If you have given the audience a big idea, pause for a second or two and let them turn it over. See what effect it has. After the smoke clears away you may have to fire another 14–inch shell on the same subject before you demolish the citadel of error that you are trying to destroy. Take time. Don't let your speech resemble those tourists who try "to do" New York in a day. They spend fifteen minutes looking at the masterpieces in the Metropolitan Museum of Arts, ten minutes in the Museum of Natural History, take a peep into the Aquarium, hurry across the Brooklyn Bridge, rush up to the Zoo, and back by Grant's Tomb—and call that "Seeing New York." If you hasten by your important points without pausing, your audience will have just about as adequate an idea of what you have tried to convey.

Take time, you have just as much of it as our richest multimillionaire. Your audience will wait for you. It is a sign of smallness to hurry. The great redwood trees of California had burst through the soil five hundred years before Socrates drank his cup of hemlock poison, and are only in their prime today. Nature shames us with our petty haste. Silence is one of the most eloquent things in the world. Master it, and use it through pause.

* * * * *

In the following selections dashes have been inserted where pauses may be used effectively. Naturally, you may omit some of these and insert others without going wrong—one speaker would interpret a passage in one way, one in another; it is largely a matter of personal preference. A dozen great actors have played Hamlet well, and yet each has played the part differently. Which comes the nearest to perfection is a question of opinion. You will succeed best by daring to follow your own course—if you are individual enough to blaze an original trail.

A moment's halt—a momentary taste of being from the well amid the waste—and lo! the phantom caravan has reached—the nothing it set out from—Oh make haste!

The worldly hope men set their hearts upon—turns ashes—or it prospers;—and anon like snow upon the desert's dusty face—lighting a little hour or two—is gone.

The bird of time has but a little way to flutter,—and the bird is on the wing.

You will note that the punctuation marks have nothing to do with the pausing. You may run by a period very quickly and make a long pause where there is no kind of punctuation. Thought is greater than punctuation. It must guide you in your pauses.

A book of verses underneath the bough,—a jug of wine, a loaf of bread—and thou beside me singing in the wilderness—Oh—wilderness were paradise enow.

You must not confuse the pause for emphasis with the natural pauses that come through taking breath and phrasing. For example, note the pauses indicated in this selection from Byron:

But *hush!—hark!*—that deep sound breaks in once more,
And *nearer!—clearer!—deadlier* than before.
Arm, ARM!—it is—it is the cannon's opening roar!

It is not necessary to dwell at length upon these obvious distinctions. You will observe that in natural conversation our words are gathered into clusters or phrases, and we often pause to take breath between them. So in public speech, breathe naturally and do not talk until you must gasp for breath; nor until the audience is equally winded.

A serious word of caution must here be uttered: do not overwork the pause. To do so will make your speech heavy and stilted. And do not think that pause can transmute commonplace thoughts into great and dignified utterance. A grand manner combined with insignificant ideas is like harnessing a Hambletonian with an ass. You remember the farcical old school declamation, "A Midnight Murder," that proceeded in grandiose manner to a thrilling climax, and ended - "and relentlessly murdered—a mosquito!"

The pause, dramatically handled, always drew a laugh from the tolerant hearers. This is all very well in farce, but such anti–climax becomes painful when the speaker falls from the sublime to the ridiculous quite unintentionally. The pause, to be effective in some other manner than in that of the boomerang, must precede or follow a thought that is really worth while, or at least an idea whose bearing upon the rest of the speech is important.

William Pittenger relates in his volume, "Extempore Speech," an instance of the unconsciously farcical use of the pause by a really great American statesman and orator. "He had visited Niagara Falls and was to make an oration at Buffalo the same day, but, unfortunately, he sat too long over the wine after dinner. When he arose to speak, the oratorical instinct struggled with difficulties, as he declared, 'Gentlemen, I have been to look upon your mag—mag—magnificent cataract, one hundred—and forty—seven—feet high! Gentlemen, Greece and Rome in their palmiest days never had a cataract one hundred—and forty—seven—feet high!'"

QUESTIONS AND EXERCISES

1. Name four methods for destroying monotony and gaining power in speaking.

2. What are the four special effects of pause?

3. Note the pauses in a conversation, play, or speech. Were they the best that could have been used? Illustrate.

4. Read aloud selections on pages 50–54, paying special attention to pause.

5. Read the following without making any pauses. Reread correctly and note the difference:

Soon the night will pass; and when, of the Sentinel on the ramparts of Liberty the anxious ask: | "Watchman, what of the night?" his answer will be | "Lo, the morn appeareth."

Knowing the price we must pay, | the sacrifice | we must make, | the burdens | we must carry, | the assaults | we must endure, | knowing full well the cost, | yet we enlist, and we enlist | for the war. | For we know the justice of our cause, | and we know, too, its certain triumph. |

Not reluctantly, then, | but eagerly, | not with faint hearts, | but strong, do we now advance upon the enemies of the people. | For the call that comes to us is the call that came to our fathers. | As they responded, so shall we.

"He hath sounded forth a trumpet | that shall never call retreat, He is sifting out the hearts of men | before His judgment seat. Oh, be swift | our souls to answer Him, | be jubilant our feet, Our God | is marching on."

—ALBERT J. BEVERIDGE, _From his speech as temporary chairman of Progressive National Convention, Chicago, 1912_.

6. Bring out the contrasting ideas in the following by using the pause:

Contrast now the circumstances of your life and mine, gently and with temper, Æschines; and then ask these people whose fortune they would each of them prefer. You taught reading, I went to school: you performed initiations, I received them: you danced in the chorus, I furnished it: you were assembly–clerk, I was a speaker: you acted third parts, I heard you: you broke down, and I hissed: you have worked as a statesman for the enemy, I for my country. I pass by the rest; but this very day I am on my probation for a crown, and am acknowledged to be innocent of all offence; while you are already judged to be a pettifogger, and the question is, whether you shall continue that trade, or at once be silenced by not getting a fifth part of the votes. A happy fortune, do you see, you have enjoyed, that you should denounce mine as miserable!

—DEMOSTHENES.

7. After careful study and practice, mark the pauses in the following:

The past rises before me like a dream. Again we are in the great struggle for national life. We hear the sounds of preparation—the music of the boisterous drums, the silver voices of heroic bugles. We see thousands of assemblages, and hear the appeals of orators; we see the pale cheeks of women and the flushed faces of men; and in those assemblages we see all the dead whose dust we have covered with flowers. We lose sight of them no more. We are with them when they enlist in the great army of freedom. We see them part from those they love. Some are walking for the last time in quiet woody places with the maiden they adore. We hear the whisperings and the sweet vows of eternal love as they lingeringly part forever. Others are bending over cradles, kissing babies that are asleep. Some are receiving the blessings of old men. Some are parting from those who hold them and press them to their hearts again and again, and say nothing; and some are talking with wives, and endeavoring with brave words spoken in the old tones to drive from their hearts the awful fear. We see them part. We see the wife standing in the door, with the babe in her arms—standing in the sunlight sobbing; at the turn of the road a hand waves—she answers by holding high in her loving hands the child. He is gone—and forever.

—ROBERT J. INGERSOLL, *to the Soldiers of Indianapolis.*

8. Where would you pause in the following selections? Try pausing in different places and note the effect it gives.

The moving finger writes; and having writ moves on: nor all your piety nor wit shall lure it back to cancel half a line, nor all your tears wash out a word of it.

The history of womankind is a story of abuse. For ages men beat, sold, and abused their wives and daughters like cattle. The Spartan mother that gave birth to one of her own sex disgraced herself; the girl babies were often deserted in the mountains to starve; China bound and deformed their feet; Turkey veiled their faces; America denied them equal educational advantages with men. Most of the world still refuses them the right to participate in the government and everywhere women bear the brunt of an unequal standard of morality.

But the women are on the march. They are walking upward to the sunlit plains where the thinking people rule. China has ceased binding their feet. In the shadow of the Harem Turkey has opened a school for girls. America has given the women equal educational advantages, and America, we believe, will enfranchise them.

We can do little to help and not much to hinder this great movement. The thinking people have put their O.K. upon it. It is moving forward to its goal just as surely as this old earth is swinging from the grip of winter toward the spring's blossoms and the summer's harvest.[1]

9. Read aloud the following address, paying careful attention to pause wherever the emphasis may thereby be heightened.

THE IRREPRESSIBLE CONFLICT

... At last, the Republican party has appeared. It avows, now, as the Republican party of 1800 did, in one word, its faith and its works, "Equal and exact justice to all men." Even when it first entered the field, only half organized, it struck a blow which only just failed to secure complete and triumphant victory. In this, its second campaign, it has already won advantages which render that triumph now both easy and certain. The secret of its assured success lies in that very characteristic which, in the mouth of scoffers, constitutes its great and lasting imbecility and reproach. It lies in the fact that it is a party of one idea; but that is a noble one—an idea that fills and expands all generous souls;

the idea of equality of all men before human tribunals and human laws, as they all are equal before the Divine tribunal and Divine laws.

I know, and you know, that a revolution has begun. I know, and all the world knows, that revolutions never go backward. Twenty senators and a hundred representatives proclaim boldly in Congress to–day sentiments and opinions and principles of freedom which hardly so many men, even in this free State, dared to utter in their own homes twenty years ago. While the government of the United States, under the conduct of the Democratic party, has been all that time surrendering one plain and castle after another to slavery, the people of the United States have been no less steadily and perseveringly gathering together the forces with which to recover back again all the fields and all the castles which have been lost, and to confound and overthrow, by one decisive blow, the betrayers of the Constitution and freedom forever.

—W.H. SEWARD.

7. Efficiency Through Inflection

How soft the music of those village bells,
Falling at intervals upon the ear
In cadence sweet; now dying all away,
Now pealing loud again, and louder still,
Clear and sonorous, as the gale comes on!
With easy force it opens all the cells
Where Memory slept.

—WILLIAM COWPER, *The Task*.

Herbert Spencer remarked that "Cadence"—by which he meant the modulation of the tones of the voice in speaking - "is the running commentary of the emotions upon the propositions of the intellect." How true this is will appear when we reflect that the little upward and downward shadings of the voice tell more truly what we mean than our words. The expressiveness of language is literally multiplied by this subtle power to shade the vocal tones, and this voice–shading we call *inflection*.

The change of pitch *within* a word is even more important, because more delicate, than the change of pitch from phrase to phrase. Indeed, one cannot be practised without the other. The bare words are only so many bricks—inflection will make of them a pavement, a garage, or a cathedral. It is the power of inflection to change the meaning of words that gave birth to the old saying: "It is not so much what you say, as how you say it."

Mrs. Jameson, the Shakespearean commentator, has given us a penetrating example of the effect of inflection; "In her impersonation of the part of Lady Macbeth, Mrs. Siddons adopted successively three different intonations in giving the words 'We fail.' At first a quick contemptuous interrogation—'We fail?' Afterwards, with the note of admiration—'We fail,' an accent of indignant astonishment laying the principal emphasis on the word 'we'—'we fail.' Lastly, she fixed on what I am convinced is the true reading—*We fail*—with the simple period, modulating the voice to a deep, low, resolute tone which settles the issue at once as though she had said: 'If we fail, why then we fail, and all is over.'"

This most expressive element of our speech is the last to be mastered in attaining to naturalness in speaking a foreign language, and its correct use is the main element in a natural, flexible utterance of our native tongue. Without varied inflections speech becomes wooden and monotonous.

There are but two kinds of inflection, the rising and the falling, yet these two may be so shaded or so combined that they are capable of producing as many varieties of modulation as maybe illustrated by either one or two lines, straight or curved, thus:

Sharp rising
Long rising
Level
Long falling
Sharp falling
Sharp rising and falling
Sharp falling and rising
Hesitating

These may be varied indefinitely, and serve merely to illustrate what wide varieties of combination may be effected by these two simple inflections of the voice.

It is impossible to tabulate the various inflections which serve to express various shades of thought and feeling. A few suggestions are offered here, together with abundant exercises for practise, but the only real way to master inflection is to observe, experiment, and practise.

For example, take the common sentence, "Oh, he's all right." Note how a rising inflection may be made to express faint praise, or polite doubt, or uncertainty of opinion. Then note how the same words, spoken with a generally falling inflection may denote certainty, or good–natured approval, or enthusiastic praise, and so on.

In general, then, we find that a bending upward of the voice will suggest doubt and uncertainty, while a decided falling inflection will suggest that you are certain of your ground.

Students dislike to be told that their speeches are "not so bad," spoken with a rising inflection. To enunciate these words with a long falling inflection would indorse the speech rather heartily.

Say good–bye to an imaginary person whom you expect to see again tomorrow; then to a dear friend you never expect to meet again. Note the difference in inflection.

"I have had a delightful time," when spoken at the termination of a formal tea by a frivolous woman takes altogether different inflection than the same words spoken between lovers who have enjoyed themselves. Mimic the two characters in repeating this and observe the difference.

Note how light and short the inflections are in the following brief quotation from "Anthony the Absolute," by Samuel Mervin.

At Sea—March 28th.

This evening I told Sir Robert What's His Name he was a fool.

I was quite right in this. He is.

Every evening since the ship left Vancouver he has presided over the round table in the middle of the smoking–room. There he sips his coffee and liqueur, and holds forth on every subject known to the mind of man. Each subject is *his* subject. He is an elderly person, with a bad face and a drooping left eyelid.

They tell me that he is in the British Service—a judge somewhere down in Malaysia, where they drink more than is good for them.

Deliver the two following selections with great earnestness, and note how the inflections differ from the foregoing. Then reread these selections in a light, superficial manner, noting that the change of attitude is expressed through a change of inflection.

When I read a sublime fact in Plutarch, or an unselfish deed in a line of poetry, or thrill beneath some heroic legend, it is no longer fairyland—I have seen it matched.

—WENDELL PHILLIPS.

Thought is deeper than all speech,

Feeling deeper than all thought;
Souls to souls can never teach
What unto themselves was taught.

—CRANCH

It must be made perfectly clear that inflection deals mostly in subtle, delicate shading *within single words*, and is not by any means accomplished by a general rise or fall in the voice in speaking a sentence. Yet certain sentences may be effectively delivered with just such inflection. Try this sentence in several ways, making no modulation until you come to the last two syllables, as indicated,

(high) And yet I told him dis– (low) tinctly.

(low) And yet I told him dis– (high) tinctly.

Now try this sentence by inflecting the important words so as to bring out various shades of meaning. The first forms, illustrated above, show change of pitch *within a single word*; the forms you will work out for yourself should show a number of such inflections throughout the sentence.

One of the chief means of securing emphasis is to employ a long falling inflection on the emphatic words—that is, to let the voice fall to a lower pitch on an *interior* vowel sound in a word. Try it on the words "every," "eleemosynary," and "destroy."

Use long falling inflections on the italicized words in the following selection, noting their emphatic power. Are there any other words here that long falling inflections would help to make expressive?

ADDRESS IN THE DARTMOUTH COLLEGE CASE

This, sir, is my case. It is the case not merely of that humble institution; it is the case of *every* college in our land. It is *more*; it is the case of *every eleemosynary* institution throughout our country—of *all* those great charities founded by the piety of our ancestors to alleviate human misery and scatter blessings along the pathway of life. Sir, you may *destroy* this little institution—it is *weak*, it is in your hands. I know it is one of the lesser lights in the literary horizon of our country. You may put it out. But if you do you must carry through your work; you must extinguish, one after another, *all* those great lights of science which, for more than a century, have thrown their radiance over our land!

It is, sir, as I have said, a small college, and yet—there are those who *love* it!

Sir, I know not how others may feel, but as for myself when I see my alma mater surrounded, like Cæsar in the senate house, by those who are reiterating *stab* after *stab*, I would not for this right hand have her turn to me and say, And *thou, too,* my son!

—DANIEL WEBSTER.

Be careful not to over–inflect. Too much modulation produces an unpleasant effect of artificiality, like a mature matron trying to be kittenish. It is a short step between true expression and unintentional burlesque. Scrutinize your own tones. Take a single expression like "Oh, no!" or "Oh, I see," or "Indeed," and by patient self–examination see how many shades of meaning may be expressed by inflection. This sort of common–sense practise will do you more good than a book of rules. *But don't forget to listen to your own voice.*

QUESTIONS AND EXERCISES

1. In your own words define (a) cadence, (b) modulation, (c) inflection, (d) emphasis.

2. Name five ways of destroying monotony and gaining effectiveness in speech.

3. What states of mind does falling inflection signify? Make as full a list as you can.

4. Do the same for the rising inflection.

5. How does the voice bend in expressing (*a*) surprise? (*b*) shame? (*c*) hate? (*d*) formality? (*e*) excitement?

6. Reread some sentence several times and by using different inflections change the meaning with each reading.

7. Note the inflections employed in some speech or conversation. Were they the best that could be used to bring out the meaning?

Criticise and illustrate.

8. Render the following passages:

Has the gentleman done? Has he completely done?

And God said, Let there be light: and there was light.

9. Invent an indirect question and show how it would naturally be inflected.

10. Does a direct question always require a rising inflection? Illustrate.

11. Illustrate how the complete ending of an expression or of a speech is indicated by inflection.

12. Do the same for incompleteness of idea.

13. Illustrate (*a*) trembling, (*b*) hesitation, and (*c*) doubt by means of inflection.

14. Show how contrast may be expressed.

15. Try the effects of both rising and falling inflections on the italicized words in the following sentences. State your preference.

Gentlemen, I am *persuaded*, nay, I am *resolved* to speak.

It is sown a *natural* body; it is raised a *spiritual* body.

SELECTIONS FOR PRACTISE

In the following selections secure emphasis by means of long falling inflections rather than loudness.

Repeat these selections, attempting to put into practise all the technical principles that we have thus far had; emphasizing important words, subordinating unimportant words, variety of pitch, changing tempo, pause, and inflection. If these principles are applied you will have no trouble with monotony.

Constant practise will give great facility in the use of inflection and will render the voice itself flexible.

CHARLES I

We charge him with having broken his coronation oath; and we are told that he kept his marriage vow! We accuse him of having given up his people to the merciless inflictions of the most hot–headed and hard–hearted of prelates; and the defence is, that he took his little son on his knee and kissed him! We censure him for having violated the articles of the Petition of Right, after having, for good and valuable consideration, promised to observe them; and we are informed that he was accustomed to hear prayers at six o'clock in the morning! It is to such considerations as these, together with his Vandyke dress, his handsome face, and his peaked beard, that he owes, we verily believe, most of his popularity with the present generation.

—T.B. MACAULAY.

ABRAHAM LINCOLN

We needed not that he should put on paper that he believed in slavery, who, with treason, with murder, with cruelty infernal, hovered around that majestic man to destroy his life. He was himself but the long sting with which slavery struck at liberty; and he carried the poison that belonged to slavery. As long as this nation lasts, it will never be forgotten that we have one martyred President—never! Never, while time lasts, while heaven lasts, while hell rocks and groans, will it be forgotten that slavery, by its minions, slew him, and in slaying him made manifest its whole nature and tendency.

But another thing for us to remember is that this blow was aimed at the life of the government and of the nation. Lincoln was slain; America was meant. The man was cast down; the government was smitten at. It was the President who was killed. It was national life, breathing freedom and meaning beneficence, that was sought. He, the man of Illinois, the private man, divested of robes and the insignia of authority, representing nothing but his personal self, might have been hated; but that would not have called forth the murderer's blow. It was because he stood in the place of government, representing government and a government that represented right and liberty, that he was singled out.

This, then, is a crime against universal government. It is not a blow at the foundations of our government, more than at the foundations of the English government, of the French government, of every compact and well–organized government. It was a crime against mankind. The whole world will repudiate and stigmatize it as a deed without a shade of redeeming light....

The blow, however, has signally failed. The cause is not stricken; it is strengthened. This nation has dissolved,—but in tears only. It stands, four–square, more solid, to–day, than any pyramid in Egypt. This people are neither wasted, nor daunted, nor disordered. Men hate slavery and love liberty with stronger hate and love to–day than ever before. The Government is not weakened, it is made stronger....

And now the martyr is moving in triumphal march, mightier than when alive. The nation rises up at every stage of his coming. Cities and states are his pall–bearers, and the cannon beats the hours with solemn progression. Dead—dead—dead—he yet speaketh! Is Washington dead? Is Hampden dead? Is David dead? Is any man dead that ever was fit to live? Disenthralled of flesh, and risen to the unobstructed sphere where passion never comes, he begins his illimitable work. His life now is grafted upon the Infinite, and will be fruitful as no earthly life can be. Pass on, thou that hast overcome! Your sorrows O people, are his peace! Your bells, and bands, and muffled drums sound triumph in his ear. Wail and weep here; God makes it echo joy and triumph there. Pass on, victor!

Four years ago, O Illinois, we took from your midst an untried man, and from among the people; we return him to you a mighty conqueror. Not thine any more, but the nation's; not ours, but the world's. Give him place, ye prairies! In the midst of this great Continent his dust shall rest, a sacred treasure to myriads who shall make pilgrimage to that shrine to kindle anew their zeal and patriotism. Ye winds, that move over the mighty places of the West, chant his requiem! Ye people, behold a martyr, whose blood, as so many inarticulate words, pleads for fidelity, for law, for liberty!

—HENRY WARD BEECHER.

THE HISTORY OF LIBERTY

The event which we commemorate is all–important, not merely in our own annals, but in those of the world. The sententious English poet has declared that "the proper study of mankind is man," and of all inquiries of a temporal nature, the history of our fellow–beings is unquestionably among the most interesting. But not all the chapters of human history are alike important. The annals of our race have been filled up with incidents which concern not, or at least ought not to concern, the great company of mankind. History, as it has often been written, is the genealogy of princes, the field–book of conquerors; and the fortunes of our fellow–men have been treated only so far as they have been affected by the influence of the great masters and destroyers of our race. Such history is, I will not say a worthless study, for it is necessary for us to know the dark side as well as the bright side of our condition. But it is a melancholy study which fills the bosom of the philanthropist and the friend of liberty with sorrow.

But the history of liberty—the history of men struggling to be free—the history of men who have acquired and are exercising their freedom—the history of those great movements in the world, by which liberty has been established and perpetuated, forms a subject which we cannot contemplate too closely. This is the real history of man, of the human family, of rational immortal beings....

The trial of adversity was theirs; the trial of prosperity is ours. Let us meet it as men who know their duty and prize their blessings. Our position is the most enviable, the most responsible, which men can fill. If this generation does its duty, the cause of constitutional freedom is safe. If we fail—if we fail—not only do we defraud our children of the inheritance which we received from our fathers, but we blast the hopes of the friends of liberty throughout our continent, throughout Europe, throughout the world, to the end of time.

History is not without her examples of hard–fought fields, where the banner of liberty has floated triumphantly on the wildest storm of battle. She is without her examples of a people by whom the dear–bought treasure has been wisely employed and safely handed down. The eyes of the world are turned for that example to us....

Let us, then, as we assemble on the birthday of the nation, as we gather upon the green turf, once wet with precious blood—let us devote ourselves to the sacred cause of constitutional liberty!

Let us abjure the interests and passions which divide the great family of American freemen!

Let the rage of party spirit sleep to–day!

Let us resolve that our children shall have cause to bless the memory of their fathers, as we have cause to bless the memory of ours!

—EDWARD EVERETT.

8. Concentration In Delivery

Attention is the microscope of the mental eye. Its power may be high or low; its field of view narrow or broad. When high power is used attention is confined within very circumscribed limits, but its action is exceedingly intense and absorbing. It sees but few things, but these few are observed "through and through" ... Mental energy and activity, whether of perception or of thought, thus concentrated, act like the sun's rays concentrated by the burning glass. The object is illumined, heated, set on fire. Impressions are so deep that they can never be effaced. Attention of this sort is the prime condition of the most productive mental labor.

—DANIEL PUTNAM, *Psychology*.

Try to rub the top of your head forward and backward at the same time that you are patting your chest. Unless your powers of coördination are well developed you will find it confusing, if not impossible. The brain needs special training before it can do two or more things efficiently at the same instant. It may seem like splitting a hair between its north and northwest corner, but some psychologists argue that *no* brain can think two distinct thoughts, absolutely simultaneously—that what seems to be simultaneous is really very rapid rotation from the first thought to the second and back again, just as in the above–cited experiment the attention must shift from one hand to the other until one or the other movement becomes partly or wholly automatic.

Whatever is the psychological truth of this contention it is undeniable that the mind measurably loses grip on one idea the moment the attention is projected decidedly ahead to a second or a third idea.

A fault in public speakers that is as pernicious as it is common is that they try to think of the succeeding sentence while still uttering the former, and in this way their concentration trails off; in consequence, they start their sentences strongly and end them weakly. In a well–prepared written speech the emphatic word usually comes at one end of the sentence. But an emphatic word needs emphatic expression, and this is precisely what it does not get when concentration flags by leaping too soon to that which is next to be uttered. Concentrate all your mental energies on the present sentence. Remember that the mind of your audience follows yours very closely, and if you withdraw your attention from what you are saying to what you are going to say, your audience will also withdraw theirs. They may not do so consciously and deliberately, but they will surely cease to give importance to the things that you yourself slight. It is fatal to either the actor or the speaker to cross his bridges too soon.

Of course, all this is not to say that in the natural pauses of your speech you are not to take swift forward surveys—they are as important as the forward look in driving a motor car; the caution is of quite another sort: *while speaking one sentence do not think of the sentence to follow*. Let it come from its proper source—within yourself. You cannot deliver a broadside without concentrated force—that is what produces the explosion. In preparation you store and concentrate thought and feeling; in the pauses during delivery you swiftly look ahead and gather yourself for effective attack; during the moments of actual speech, *SPEAK—DON'T ANTICIPATE.* Divide your attention and you divide your power.

This matter of the effect of the inner man upon the outer needs a further word here, particularly as touching concentration.

"What do you read, my lord?" Hamlet replied, "Words. Words. Words." That is a world–old trouble. The mechanical calling of words is not expression, by a long stretch. Did you ever notice how hollow a memorized speech usually sounds? You have listened to the ranting, mechanical cadence of inefficient actors, lawyers and preachers. Their trouble is a mental one—they are not concentratedly thinking thoughts that cause words to issue with sincerity and conviction, but are merely enunciating word–sounds mechanically. Painful experience alike to audience and to speaker! A parrot is equally eloquent. Again let Shakespeare instruct us, this tune in the insincere prayer of the King, Hamlet's uncle. He laments thus pointedly:

My words fly up, my thoughts remain below:
Words without thoughts never to heaven go.

The truth is, that as a speaker your words must be born again every time they are spoken, then they will not suffer in their utterance, even though perforce committed to memory and repeated, like Dr. Russell Conwell's lecture, "Acres of Diamonds," five thousand times. Such speeches lose nothing by repetition for the perfectly patent reason that they arise from concentrated thought and feeling and not a mere necessity for saying something—which usually means anything, and that, in turn, is tantamount to nothing. If the thought beneath your words is warm, fresh, spontaneous, a part of your*self*, your utterance will have breath and life. Words are only a result. Do not try to get the result without stimulating the cause.

Do you ask *how* to concentrate? Think of the word itself, and of its philological brother, *concentric*. Think of how a lens gathers and con-centers the rays of light within a given circle. It centers them by a process of withdrawal. It may seem like a harsh saying, but the man who cannot concentrate is either weak of will, a nervous wreck, or has never learned what will–power is good for.

You must concentrate by resolutely withdrawing your attention from everything else. If you concentrate your thought on a pain which may be afflicting you, that pain will grow more intense. "Count your bless-ings" and they will multiply. Center your thought on your strokes and your tennis play will gradually improve. To concentrate is simply to attend to one thing, and attend to nothing else. If you find that you cannot do that, there is something wrong—attend to that first. Re-move the cause and the symptom will disappear. Read the chapter on "Will Power." Cultivate your will by willing and then doing, at all costs. Concentrate—and you will win.

QUESTIONS AND EXERCISES

1. Select from any source several sentences suitable for speaking aloud; deliver them first in the manner condemned in this chapter, and second with due regard for emphasis toward the close of each sentence.

2. Put into about one hundred words your impression of the effect produced.

3. Tell of any peculiar methods you may have observed or heard of by which speakers have sought to aid their powers of concentration, such as looking fixedly at a blank spot in the ceiling, or twisting a watch

charm.

4. What effect do such habits have on the audience?

5. What relation does pause bear to concentration?

6. Tell why concentration naturally helps a speaker to change pitch, tempo, and emphasis.

7. Read the following selection through to get its meaning and spirit clearly in your mind. Then read it aloud, concentrating solely on the thought that you are expressing—do not trouble about the sentence or thought that is coming. Half the troubles of mankind arise from anticipating trials that never occur. Avoid this in speaking. Make the end of your sentences just as strong as the beginning. *CONCENTRATE.*

WAR!

The last of the savage instincts is war. The cave man's club made law and procured food. Might decreed right. Warriors were saviours.

In Nazareth a carpenter laid down the saw and preached the brotherhood of man. Twelve centuries afterwards his followers marched to the Holy Land to destroy all who differed with them in the worship of the God of Love. Triumphantly they wrote "In Solomon's Porch and in his temple our men rode in the blood of the Saracens up to the knees of their horses."

History is an appalling tale of war. In the seventeenth century Germany, France, Sweden, and Spain warred for thirty years. At Magdeburg 30,000 out of 36,000 were killed regardless of sex or age. In Germany schools were closed for a third of a century, homes burned, women outraged, towns demolished, and the untilled land became a wilderness.

Two–thirds of Germany's property was destroyed and 18,000,000 of her citizens were killed, because men quarrelled about the way to glorify "The Prince of Peace." Marching through rain and snow, sleeping on the ground, eating stale food or starving, contracting diseases and facing guns that fire six hundred times a minute, for fifty cents a day—this is the soldier's life.

At the window sits the widowed mother crying. Little children with tearful faces pressed against the pane watch and wait. Their means of livelihood, their home, their happiness is gone. Fatherless children, broken–hearted women, sick, disabled and dead men—this is the wage of war.

We spend more money preparing men to kill each other than we do in teaching them to live. We spend more money building one battleship than in the annual maintenance of all our state universities. The financial loss resulting from destroying one another's homes in the civil war would have built 15,000,000 houses, each costing $2,000. We pray for love but prepare for hate. We preach peace but equip for war.

Were half the power that fills the world with terror,
Were half the wealth bestowed on camp and court
Given to redeem this world from error,
There would be no need of arsenal and fort.

War only defers a question. No issue will ever really be settled until it is settled rightly. Like rival "gun gangs" in a back alley, the nations of the world, through the bloody ages, have fought over their differences. Denver cannot fight Chicago and Iowa cannot fight Ohio. Why should Germany be permitted to fight France, or Bulgaria fight Turkey?

When mankind rises above creeds, colors and countries, when we are citizens, not of a nation, but of the world, the armies and navies of the earth will constitute an international police force to preserve the peace and the dove will take the eagle's place.

Our differences will be settled by an international court with the power to enforce its mandates. In times of peace prepare for peace. The wages of war are the wages of sin, and the "wages of sin is death."

—*Editorial by D.C., Leslie's Weekly; used by permission.*

9. Force

However, 'tis expedient to be wary:
Indifference, certes, don't produce distress;
And rash enthusiasm in good society
Were nothing but a moral inebriety.

—BYRON, *Don Juan.*

You have attended plays that seemed fair, yet they did not move you, grip you. In theatrical parlance, they failed to "get over," which means that their message did not get over the foot–lights to the audience. There was no punch, no jab to them—they had no force.

Of course, all this spells disaster, in big letters, not only in a stage production but in any platform effort. Every such presentation exists solely for the audience, and if it fails to hit them—and the expression is a good one—it has no excuse for living; nor will it live long.

What is Force?

Some of our most obvious words open up secret meanings under scrutiny, and this is one of them.

To begin with, we must recognize the distinction between inner and outer force. The one is cause, the other effect. The one is spiritual, the other physical. In this important particular, animate force differs from inanimate force—the power of man, coming from within and expressing itself outwardly, is of another sort from the force of Shimose powder, which awaits some influence from without to explode it. However susceptive to outside stimuli, the true source of power in man lies within himself. This may seem like "mere psychology," but it has an intensely practical bearing on public speaking, as will appear.

Not only must we discern the difference between human force and mere physical force, but we must not confuse its real essence with some of the things that may—and may not—accompany it. For example, loudness is not force, though force at times may be attended by noise. Mere roaring never made a good speech, yet there are moments—moments, mind you, not minutes—when big voice power may be used with tremendous effect.

Nor is violent motion force—yet force may result in violent motion. Hamlet counseled the players:

Nor do not saw the air too much with your hand, thus; but use all gently; for in the very torrent, tempest, and (as I may say) whirlwind of your passion, you must acquire and beget a temperance, that may give it smoothness. Oh, it offends me to the soul, to hear a robustious periwig–pated fellow tear a passion to tatters, to very rags, to split the ears of the groundlings[2]; who, for the most part, are capable of nothing but inexplicable dumb show, and noise. I would have such a fellow whipped for o'er–doing Termagant; it out–herods Herod. Pray you avoid it.

Be not too tame, neither, but let your discretion be your tutor: suit the action to the word, the word to the action; with this special observance, that you o'erstep not the modesty of nature; for anything so overdone is from the purpose of playing, whose end, both at the first, and now, was, and is, to hold, as 'twere, the mirror up to Nature, to show Virtue her own feature, Scorn her own image, and the very age and body of the time his form and pressure. Now, this overdone, or come tardy off, though it make the unskillful laugh, cannot but make the judicious grieve; the censure of the which one must, in your allowance, o'erweigh a whole theater of others. Oh, there be players that I have seen play—and heard others praise, and that highly—not to speak it profanely, that, neither having the accent of Christians, nor the gait of Christian, pagan, or man, have so strutted and bellowed that I have thought some of Nature's journeymen had made men, and not made them well, they imitated humanity so abominably.[3]

Force is both a cause and an effect. Inner force, which must precede outer force, is a combination of four elements, acting progressively. First of all, *force arises from conviction*. You must be convinced of the truth, or the importance, or the meaning, of what you are about to say before you can give it forceful delivery. It must lay strong hold upon your convictions before it can grip your audience. Conviction convinces.

The Saturday Evening Post in an article on "England's T.R."—Winston

Spencer Churchill—attributed much of Churchill's and Roosevelt's public platform success to their forceful delivery. No matter what is in hand, these men make themselves believe for the time being that that one thing is the most important on earth. Hence they speak to their audiences in a Do–this–or–you–*PERISH* manner.

That kind of speaking wins, and it is that virile, strenuous, aggressive attitude which both distinguishes and maintains the platform careers of our greatest leaders.

But let us look a little closer at the origins of inner force. How does conviction affect the man who feels it? We have answered the inquiry in the very question itself—he *feels* it: *Conviction produces emotional tension.* Study the pictures of Theodore Roosevelt and of Billy Sunday in action—*action* is the word. Note the tension of their jaw muscles, the taut lines of sinews in their entire bodies when reaching a climax of force. Moral and physical force are alike in being both preceded and accompanied by in–*tens*–ity—tension—tightness of the cords of power.

It is this tautness of the bow–string, this knotting of the muscles, this contraction before the spring, that makes an audience *feel*—almost see—the reserve power in a speaker. In some really wonderful way it is more what a speaker does *not* say and do that reveals the dynamo within. *Anything* may come from such stored–up force once it is let loose; and that keeps an audience alert, hanging on the lips of a speaker for his next word. After all, it is all a question of manhood, for a stuffed doll has neither convictions nor emotional tension. If you are upholstered with sawdust, keep off the platform, for your own speech will puncture you.

Growing out of this conviction–tension comes *resolve to make the audience share that conviction–tension.* Purpose is the backbone of force; without it speech is flabby—it may glitter, but it is the iridescence of the spineless jellyfish. You must hold fast to your resolve if you would hold fast to your audience.

Finally, all this conviction–tension–purpose is lifeless and useless unless it results in *propulsion.* You remember how Young in his wonderful "Night Thoughts" delineates the man who

Pushes   his   prudent   purpose   to   resolve,
Resolves, and re–resolves, and dies the same.

Let not your force "die a–borning,"—bring it to full life in its conviction, emotional tension, resolve, and propulsive power.

Can Force be Acquired?

Yes, if the acquirer has any such capacities as we have just outlined. How to acquire this vital factor is suggested in its very analysis: Live with your subject until you are convinced of its importance.

If your message does not of itself arouse you to tension, *PULL* yourself together. When a man faces the necessity of leaping across a crevasse he does not wait for inspiration, he *wills* his muscles into tensity for the spring—it is not without purpose that our English language uses the same word to depict a mighty though delicate steel contrivance and a quick leap through the air. Then resolve—and let it all end in actual *punch*.

This truth is worth reiteration: The man within is the final factor. He must supply the fuel. The audience, or even the man himself, may add the match—it matters little which, only so that there be fire. However skillfully your engine is constructed, however well it works, you will have no force if the fire has gone out under the boiler. It matters little how well you have mastered poise, pause, modulation, and tempo, if your speech lacks fire it is dead. Neither a dead engine nor a dead speech will move anybody.

Four factors of force are measurably within your control, and in that far may be acquired: *ideas, feeling about the subject, wording,* and *delivery*. Each of these is more or less fully discussed in this volume, except wording, which really requires a fuller rhetorical study than can here be ventured. It is, however, of the utmost importance that you should be aware of precisely how wording bears upon force in a sentence. Study "The Working Principles of Rhetoric," by John Franklin Genung, or the rhetorical treatises of Adams Sherman Hill, of Charles Sears Baldwin, or any others whose names may easily be learned from any teacher.

Here are a few suggestions on the use of words to attain force:

Choice of Words

PLAIN words are more forceful than words less commonly used—*juggle* has more vigor than *prestidigitate.*

SHORT words are stronger than long words—*end* has more directness than *terminate.*

SAXON words are usually more forceful than Latinistic words—for force, use *wars against* rather than *militate against.*

SPECIFIC words are stronger than general words—*pressman* is more definite than *printer.*

CONNOTATIVE words, those that suggest more than they say, have more power than ordinary words - "She *let* herself be married" expresses more than "She *married.*"

EPITHETS, figuratively descriptive words, are more effective than direct names - "Go tell that *old fox,*" has more "punch" than "Go tell that *sly fellow.*" ONOMATOPOETIC words, words that convey the sense by the sound, are more powerful than other words—*crash* is more effective than *cataclysm.*

Arrangement of words

Cut out modifiers.

Cut out connectives.

Begin with words that demand attention.

"End with words that deserve distinction," says Prof. Barrett Wendell.

Set strong ideas over against weaker ones, so as to gain strength by the contrast.

Avoid elaborate sentence structure—short sentences are stronger than long ones.

Cut out every useless word, so as to give prominence to the really important ones.

Let each sentence be a condensed battering ram, swinging to its final blow on the attention.

A familiar, homely idiom, if not worn by much use, is more effective than a highly formal, scholarly expression.

Consider well the relative value of different positions in the sentence so that you may give the prominent place to ideas you wish to emphasize.

"But," says someone, "is it not more honest to depend the inherent interest in a subject, its native truth, clearness and sincerity of presentation, and beauty of utterance, to win your audience? Why not charm men instead of capturing them by assault?"

Why Use Force?

There is much truth in such an appeal, but not all the truth. Clearness, persuasion, beauty, simple statement of truth, are all essential—indeed, they are all definite parts of a forceful presentment of a subject, without being the only parts. Strong meat may not be as attractive as ices, but all depends on the appetite and the stage of the meal.

You can not deliver an aggressive message with caressing little strokes. No! Jab it in with hard, swift solar plexus punches. You cannot strike fire from flint or from an audience with love taps. Say to a crowded theatre in a lackadaisical manner: "It seems to me that the house is on fire," and your announcement may be greeted with a laugh. If you flash out the words: "The house's on fire!" they will crush one another in getting to the exits.

The spirit and the language of force are definite with conviction. No immortal speech in literature contains such expressions as "it seems to me," "I should judge," "in my opinion," "I suppose," "perhaps it is true." The speeches that will live have been delivered by men ablaze with the courage of their convictions, who uttered their words as eternal truth. Of Jesus it was said that "the common people heard Him gladly." Why? "He taught them as one having *AUTHORITY*." An audience will never be moved by what "seems" to you to be truth or what in your "humble opinion" may be so. If you honestly can, assert convictions as your conclusions. Be sure you are right before you speak your speech, then utter your thoughts as though they were a Gibraltar of unimpeachable *truth*. Deliver them with the iron hand and confidence of a Cromwell. Assert them with the fire of *authority*. Pronounce them as an *ultimatum*. If you cannot speak with conviction, be silent.

What force did that young minister have who, fearing to be too dogmatic, thus exhorted his hearers: "My friends—as I assume that you are—it appears to be my duty to tell you that if you do not repent, so to speak, forsake your sins, as it were, and turn to righteousness, if I may so express it, you will be lost, in a measure"?

Effective speech must reflect the era. This is not a rose water age, and a tepid, half–hearted speech will not win. This is the century of trip hammers, of overland expresses that dash under cities and through mountain tunnels, and you must instill this spirit into your speech if you would move a popular audience. From a front seat listen to a first–class company present a modern Broadway drama—not a comedy, but a gripping, thrilling drama. Do not become absorbed in the story; reserve all your attention for the technique and the force of the acting. There is a kick and a crash as well as an infinitely subtle intensity in the big, climax–speeches that suggest this lesson: the same well–calculated, restrained, delicately shaded force would simply *rivet* your ideas in the minds of your audience. An air–gun will rattle bird–shot against a window pane—it takes a rifle to wing a bullet through plate glass and the oaken walls beyond.

When to Use Force

An audience is unlike the kingdom of heaven—the violent do not always take it by force. There are times when beauty and serenity should be the only bells in your chime. Force is only one of the great extremes of contrast—use neither it nor quiet utterance to the exclusion of other tones: be various, and in variety find even greater force than you could attain by attempting its constant use. If you are reading an essay on the beauties of the dawn, talking about the dainty bloom of a honey–suckle, or explaining the mechanism of a gas engine, a vigorous style of delivery is entirely out of place. But when you are appealing to wills and consciences for immediate action, forceful delivery wins. In such cases, consider the minds of your audience as so many safes that have been locked and the keys lost. Do not try to figure out the combinations. Pour a little nitro glycerine into the cracks and light the fuse. As these lines are being written a contractor down the street is clearing away the rocks with dynamite to lay the foundations for a great building. When you want to get action, do not fear to use dynamite.

The final argument for the effectiveness of force in public speech is the fact that everything must be enlarged for the purposes of the platform—that is why so few speeches read well in the reports on the morning after: statements appear crude and exaggerated because they are unaccompanied by the forceful delivery of a glowing speaker before an audience heated to attentive enthusiasm. So in preparing your speech you must not err on the side of mild statement—your audience will inevitably tone down your words in the cold grey of afterthought. When Phidias was criticised for the rough, bold outlines of a figure he had submitted in competition, he smiled and asked that his statue and the one wrought by his rival should be set upon the column for which the sculpture was destined. When this was done all the exaggerations and crudities, toned by distances, melted into exquisite grace of line and form. Each speech must be a special study in suitability and proportion.

Omit the thunder of delivery, if you will, but like Wendell Phillips put "silent lightning" into your speech. Make your thoughts breathe and your words burn. Birrell said: "Emerson writes like an electrical cat emitting sparks and shocks in every sentence." Go thou and speak likewise. Get the "big stick" into your delivery—be forceful.

QUESTIONS AND EXERCISES

1. Illustrate, by repeating a sentence from memory, what is meant by employing force in speaking.

2. Which in your opinion is the most important of the technical principles of speaking that you have studied so far? Why?

3. What is the effect of too much force in a speech? Too little?

4. Note some uninteresting conversation or ineffective speech, and tell why it failed.

5. Suggest how it might be improved.

6. Why do speeches have to be spoken with more force than do conversations?

7. Read aloud the selection on page 84, using the technical principles outlined in chapters III to VIII, but neglect to put any force behind the

interpretation. What is the result?

8. Reread several times, doing your best to achieve force.

9. Which parts of the selection on page 84 require the most force?

10. Write a five-minute speech not only discussing the errors of those who exaggerate and those who minimize the use of force, but by imitation show their weaknesses. Do not burlesque, but closely imitate.

11. Give a list of ten themes for public addresses, saying which seem most likely to require the frequent use of force in delivery.

12. In your own opinion, do speakers usually err from the use of too much or too little force?

13. Define (a) bombast; (b) bathos; (c) sentimentality; (d) squeamish.

14. Say how the foregoing words describe weaknesses in public speech.

15. Recast in twentieth-century English "Hamlet's Directions to the Players," page 88.

16. Memorize the following extracts from Wendell Phillips' speeches, and deliver them with the of Wendell Phillips' "silent lightning" delivery.

We are for a revolution! We say in behalf of these hunted lyings, whom God created, and who law-abiding Webster and Winthrop have sworn shall not find shelter in Massachusetts,—we say that they may make their little motions, and pass their little laws in Washington, but that Faneuil Hall repeals them in the name of humanity and the old Bay State!

* * * * *

My advice to workingmen is this:

If you want power in this country; if you want to make yourselves felt; if you do not want your children to wait long years before they have the bread on the table they ought to have, the leisure in their lives they ought to have, the opportunities in life they ought to have; if you don't want to wait yourselves,—write on your banner, so that every political trimmer can read it, so that every politician, no matter how short–sighted he may be, can read it, "*WE NEVER FORGET!* If you launch the arrow of sarcasm at labor, *WE NEVER FORGET!* If there is a division in Congress, and you throw your vote in the wrong scale, *WE NEVER FORGET!* You may go down on your knees, and say, 'I am sorry I did the act'—but we will say '*IT WILL AVAIL YOU IN HEAVEN TO BE SORRY, BUT ON THIS SIDE OF THE GRAVE, NEVER!*'" So that a man in taking up the labor question will know he is dealing with a hair–trigger pistol, and will say, "I am to be true to justice and to man; otherwise I am a dead duck."

* * * * *

In Russia there is no press, no debate, no explanation of what government does, no remonstrance allowed, no agitation of public issues. Dead silence, like that which reigns at the summit of Mont Blanc, freezes the whole empire, long ago described as "a despotism tempered by assassination." Meanwhile, such despotism has unsettled the brains of the ruling family, as unbridled power doubtless made some of the twelve Cæsars insane; a madman, sporting with the lives and comfort of a hundred millions of men. The young girl whispers in her mother's ear, under a ceiled roof, her pity for a brother knouted and dragged half dead into exile for his opinions. The next week she is stripped naked and flogged to death in the public square. No inquiry, no explanation, no trial, no protest, one dead uniform silence, the law of the tyrant. Where is there ground for any hope of peaceful change? No, no! in such a land dynamite and the dagger are the necessary and proper substitutes for Faneuil Hall. Anything that will make the madman quake in his bedchamber, and rouse his victims into reckless and desperate resistance. This is the only view an American, the child of 1620 and 1776, can take of Nihilism. Any other unsettles and perplexes the ethics of our civilization.

Born within sight of Bunker Hill—son of Harvard, whose first pledge was "Truth," citizen of a republic based on the claim that no government is rightful unless resting on the consent of the people, and which assumes to lead in asserting the rights of humanity—I at least can say nothing else and nothing less—no not if every tile on Cambridge roofs were a devil hooting my words!

For practise on forceful selections, use "The Irrepressible Conflict," page 67; "Abraham Lincoln," page 76, "Pass Prosperity Around," page 470; "A Plea for Cuba," page 50.

10. Feeling And Enthusiasm

Enthusiasm is that secret and harmonious spirit that hovers over the production of genius.

—ISAAC DISRAELI, *Literary Character.*

If you are addressing a body of scientists on such a subject as the veins in a butterfly's wings, or on road structure, naturally your theme will not arouse much feeling in either you or your audience. These are purely mental subjects. But if you want men to vote for a measure that will abolish child labor, or if you would inspire them to take up arms for freedom, you must strike straight at their feelings. We lie on soft beds, sit near the radiator on a cold day, eat cherry pie, and devote our attention to one of the opposite sex, not because we have reasoned out that it is the right thing to do, but because it feels right. No one but a dyspeptic chooses his diet from a chart. Our feelings dictate what we shall eat and generally how we shall act. Man is a feeling animal, hence the public speaker's ability to arouse men to action depends almost wholly on his ability to touch their emotions.

Negro mothers on the auction–block seeing their children sold away from them into slavery have flamed out some of America's most stirring speeches. True, the mother did not have any knowledge of the technique of speaking, but she had something greater than all technique, more effective than reason: feeling. The great speeches of the world have not been delivered on tariff reductions or post–office appropriations. The speeches that will live have been charged with emotional force. Prosperity and peace are poor developers of eloquence. When great wrongs are to be righted, when the public heart is flaming with passion, that is the occasion for memorable speaking. Patrick Henry made an immortal address, for in an epochal crisis he pleaded for liberty. He had roused himself to the point where he could honestly and passionately exclaim, "Give me liberty or give me death." His fame would have been different had he lived to–day and argued for the recall of judges.

The Power of Enthusiasm

Political parties hire bands, and pay for applause—they argue that, for vote–getting, to stir up enthusiasm is more effective than reasoning. How far they are right depends on the hearers, but there can be no doubt about the contagious nature of enthusiasm. A watch manufacturer in New York tried out two series of watch advertisements; one argued the superior construction, workmanship, durability, and guarantee offered with the watch; the other was headed, "A Watch to be Proud of," and dwelt upon the pleasure and pride of ownership. The latter series sold twice as many as the former. A salesman for a locomotive works informed the writer that in selling railroad engines emotional appeal was stronger than an argument based on mechanical excellence.

Illustrations without number might be cited to show that in all our actions we are emotional beings. The speaker who would speak efficiently must develop the power to arouse feeling.

Webster, great debater that he was, knew that the real secret of a speaker's power was an emotional one. He eloquently says of eloquence:

"Affected passion, intense expression, the pomp of declamation, all may aspire after it; they cannot reach it. It comes, if it come at all, like the outbreak of a fountain from the earth, or the bursting forth of volcanic fires, with spontaneous, original, native force.

"The graces taught in the schools, the costly ornaments and studied contrivances of speech, shock and disgust men, when their own lives, and the fate of their wives, their children, and their country hang on the decision of the hour. Then words have lost their power, rhetoric is in vain, and all elaborate oratory contemptible. Even genius itself then feels rebuked and subdued, as in the presence of higher qualities. Then patriotism is eloquent, then self–devotion is eloquent. The clear conception outrunning the deductions of logic, the high purpose, the firm resolve, the dauntless spirit, speaking on the tongue, beaming from the eye, informing every feature, and urging the whole man onward, right onward to his subject—this, this is eloquence; or rather, it is something greater and higher than all eloquence; it is action, noble, sublime, godlike action."

When traveling through the Northwest some time ago, one of the present writers strolled up a village street after dinner and noticed a crowd listening to a "faker" speaking on a corner from a goods-box. Remembering Emerson's advice about learning something from every man we meet, the observer stopped to listen to this speaker's appeal. He was selling a hair tonic, which he claimed to have discovered in Arizona. He removed his hat to show what this remedy had done for him, washed his face in it to demonstrate that it was as harmless as water, and enlarged on its merits in such an enthusiastic manner that the half-dollars poured in on him in a silver flood. When he had supplied the audience with hair tonic, he asked why a greater proportion of men than women were bald. No one knew. He explained that it was because women wore thinner-soled shoes, and so made a good electrical connection with mother earth, while men wore thick, dry-soled shoes that did not transmit the earth's electricity to the body. Men's hair, not having a proper amount of electrical food, died and fell out. Of course he had a remedy—a little copper plate that should be nailed on the bottom of the shoe. He pictured in enthusiastic and vivid terms the desirability of escaping baldness—and paid tributes to his copper plates. Strange as it may seem when the story is told in cold print, the speaker's enthusiasm had swept his audience with him, and they crushed around his stand with outstretched "quarters" in their anxiety to be the possessors of these magical plates!

Emerson's suggestion had been well taken—the observer had seen again the wonderful, persuasive power of enthusiasm!

Enthusiasm sent millions crusading into the Holy Land to redeem it from the Saracens. Enthusiasm plunged Europe into a thirty years' war over religion. Enthusiasm sent three small ships plying the unknown sea to the shores of a new world. When Napoleon's army were worn out and discouraged in their ascent of the Alps, the Little Corporal stopped them and ordered the bands to play the Marseillaise. Under its soul-stirring strains there were no Alps.

Listen! Emerson said: "Nothing great was ever achieved without enthusiasm." Carlyle declared that "Every great movement in the annals of history has been the triumph of enthusiasm." It is as contagious as measles. Eloquence is half inspiration. Sweep your audience with you in a pulsation of enthusiasm. Let yourself go. "A man," said Oliver Cromwell, "never rises so high as when he knows not whither he is going."

How are We to Acquire and Develop Enthusiasm?

It is not to be slipped on like a smoking jacket. A book cannot furnish you with it. It is a growth—an effect. But an effect of what? Let us see.

Emerson wrote: "A painter told me that nobody could draw a tree without in some sort becoming a tree; or draw a child by studying the outlines of his form merely,—but, by watching for a time his motion and plays, the painter enters his nature, and then can draw him at will in every attitude. So Roos 'entered into the inmost nature of his sheep.' I knew a draughtsman employed in a public survey, who found that he could not sketch the rocks until their geological structure was first explained to him."

When Sarah Bernhardt plays a difficult role she frequently will speak to no one from four o'clock in the afternoon until after the performance. From the hour of four she lives her character. Booth, it is reported, would not permit anyone to speak to him between the acts of his Shakesperean rôles, for he was Macbeth then—not Booth. Dante, exiled from his beloved Florence, condemned to death, lived in caves, half starved; then Dante wrote out his heart in "The Divine Comedy." Bunyan entered into the spirit of his "Pilgrim's Progress" so thoroughly that he fell down on the floor of Bedford jail and wept for joy. Turner, who lived in a garret, arose before daybreak and walked over the hills nine miles to see the sun rise on the ocean, that he might catch the spirit of its wonderful beauty. Wendell Phillips' sentences were full of "silent lightning" because he bore in his heart the sorrow of five million slaves.

There is only one way to get feeling into your speaking—and whatever else you forget, forget not this: *You must actually ENTER INTO* the character you impersonate, the cause you advocate, the case you argue—enter into it so deeply that it clothes you, enthralls you, possesses you wholly. Then you are, in the true meaning of the word, in *sympathy* with your subject, for its feeling is your feeling, you "feel with" it, and therefore your enthusiasm is both genuine and contagious. The Carpenter who spoke as "never man spake" uttered words born out of a passion of love for humanity—he had entered into humanity, and thus became Man.

But we must not look upon the foregoing words as a facile prescription for decocting a feeling which may then be ladled out to a complacent audience in quantities to suit the need of the moment. Genuine feeling in a speech is bone and blood of the speech itself and not something that may be added to it or substracted at will. In the ideal address theme, speaker and audience become one, fused by the emotion and thought of the hour.

The Need of Sympathy for Humanity

It is impossible to lay too much stress on the necessity for the speaker's having a broad and deep tenderness for human nature. One of Victor Hugo's biographers attributes his power as an orator and writer to his wide sympathies and profound religious feelings. Recently we heard the editor of *Collier's Weekly* speak on short–story writing, and he so often emphasized the necessity for this broad love for humanity, this truly religious feeling, that he apologized twice for delivering a sermon. Few if any of the immortal speeches were ever delivered for a selfish or a narrow cause—they were born out of a passionate desire to help humanity; instances, Paul's address to the Athenians on Mars Hill, Lincoln's Gettysburg speech, The Sermon on the Mount, Henry's address before the Virginia Convention of Delegates.

The seal and sign of greatness is a desire to serve others. Self–preservation is the first law of life, but self–abnegation is the first law of greatness—and of art. Selfishness is the fundamental cause of all sin, it is the thing that all great religions, all worthy philosophies, have struck at. Out of a heart of real sympathy and love come the speeches that move humanity.

Former United States Senator Albert J. Beveridge in an introduction to one of the volumes of "Modern Eloquence," says: "The profoundest feeling among the masses, the most influential element in their character, is the religious element. It is as instinctive and elemental as the law of self–preservation. It informs the whole intellect and personality of the people. And he who would greatly influence the people by uttering their unformed thoughts must have this great and unanalyzable bond of sympathy with them."

When the men of Ulster armed themselves to oppose the passage of the Home Rule Act, one of the present writers assigned to a hundred men "Home Rule" as the topic for an address to be prepared by each. Among this group were some brilliant speakers, several of them experienced lawyers and political campaigners. Some of their addresses showed a remarkable knowledge and grasp of the subject; others were clothed in the most attractive phrases. But a clerk, without a great deal of education and experience, arose and told how he spent his boyhood days in Ulster, how his mother while holding him on her lap had pictured to him Ulster's deeds of valor. He spoke of a picture in his uncle's home that showed the men of Ulster conquering a tyrant and marching on to victory. His voice quivered, and with a hand pointing upward he declared that if the men of Ulster went to war they would not go alone—a great God would go with them.

The speech thrilled and electrified the audience. It thrills yet as we recall it. The high–sounding phrases, the historical knowledge, the philosophical treatment, of the other speakers largely failed to arouse any deep interest, while the genuine conviction and feeling of the modest clerk, speaking on a subject that lay deep in his heart, not only electrified his audience but won their personal sympathy for the cause he advocated.

As Webster said, it is of no use to try to pretend to sympathy or feelings. It cannot be done successfully. "Nature is forever putting a premium on reality." What is false is soon detected as such. The thoughts and feelings that create and mould the speech in the study must be born again when the speech is delivered from the platform. Do not let your words say one thing, and your voice and attitude another. There is no room here for half–hearted, nonchalant methods of delivery. Sincerity is the very soul of eloquence. Carlyle was right: "No Mirabeau, Napoleon, Burns, Cromwell, no man adequate to do anything, but is first of all in right earnest about it; what I call a sincere man. I should say sincerity, a great, deep, genuine sincerity, is the first characteristic of all men in any way heroic. Not the sincerity that calls itself sincere; ah no, that is a very poor matter indeed; a shallow braggart, conscious sincerity, oftenest self–conceit mainly. The great man's sincerity is of the kind he cannot speak of—is not conscious of."

QUESTIONS AND EXERCISES

It is one thing to convince the would–be speaker that he ought to put feeling into his speeches; often it is quite another thing for him to do it. The average speaker is afraid to let himself go, and continually suppresses his emotions. When you put enough feeling into your speeches they will sound overdone to you, unless you are an experienced speaker. They will sound too strong, if you are not used to enlarging for platform or stage, for the delineation of the emotions must be enlarged for public delivery.

1. Study the following speech, going back in your imagination to the time and circumstances that brought it forth. Make it not a memorized historical document, but feel the emotions that gave it birth. The speech is only an effect; live over in your own heart the causes that produced it and try to deliver it at white heat. It is not possible for you to put too much real feeling into it, though of course it would be quite easy to rant and fill it with false emotion. This speech, according to Thomas Jefferson, started the ball of the Revolution rolling. Men were then willing to go out and die for liberty.

PATRICK HENRY'S SPEECH

BEFORE THE VIRGINIA CONVENTION OF DELEGATES

Mr. President, it is natural to man to indulge in the illusions of hope. We are apt to shut our eyes against a painful truth, and listen to the song of that siren, till she transforms us to beasts. Is this the part of wise men, engaged in a great and arduous struggle for liberty? Are we disposed to be of the number of those who, having eyes, see not, and having ears, hear not, the things which so nearly concern our temporal salvation? For my part, whatever anguish of spirit it may cost, I am willing to know the whole truth; to know the worst, and to provide for it.

I have but one lamp by which my feet are guided; and that is the lamp of experience. I know of no way of judging of the future but by the past. And judging by the past, I wish to know what there has been in the conduct of the British Ministry for the last ten years to justify those hopes with which gentlemen have been pleased to solace themselves and the House? Is it that insidious smile with which our petition has been lately received? Trust it not, sir; it will prove a snare to your feet. Suffer not yourselves to be "betrayed with a kiss"! Ask yourselves, how this gracious reception of our petition comports with those warlike preparations which cover our waters and darken our land. Are fleets and armies necessary to a work of love and reconciliation? Have we shown ourselves so unwilling to be reconciled, that force must be called in to win back our love? Let us not deceive ourselves, sir. These are the implements of war and subjugation, the last "arguments" to which kings resort.

I ask gentlemen, sir, what means this martial array, if its purpose be not to force us to submission? Can gentlemen assign any other possible motive for it? Has Great Britain any enemy in this quarter of the world, to call for all this accumulation of navies and armies? No, sir, she has none. They are meant for us; they can be meant for no other. They are sent over to bind and to rivet upon us those chains which the British Ministry have been so long forging. And what have we to oppose to them? Shall we try argument? Sir, we have been trying that for the last ten years. Have we anything new to offer upon the subject? Nothing. We have held the subject up in every light of which it is capable; but it has been all in vain. Shall we resort to entreaty and humble supplication? What terms shall we find which have not been already exhausted? Let us not, I beseech you, sir, deceive ourselves longer. Sir, we have done everything that could be done, to avert the storm which is now coming on. We have petitioned, we have remonstrated, we have supplicated, we have prostrated ourselves before the throne, and have implored its interposition to arrest the tyrannical hands of the Ministry and Parliament. Our petitions have been slighted; our remonstrances have produced additional violence and insult; our supplications have been disregarded, and we have been spurned with contempt from the foot of the throne. In vain, after these things, may we indulge in the fond hope of peace and reconciliation. There is no longer any room for hope. If we wish to be free, if we mean to preserve inviolate those inestimable privileges for which we have been so long contending; if we mean not basely to abandon the noble struggle in which we have been so long engaged, and which we have pledged ourselves never to abandon until the glorious object of our contest shall be obtained, we must fight; I repeat it, sir, we must fight! An appeal to arms, and to the God of Hosts, is all that is left us!

They tell us, sir, that we are weak - "unable to cope with so formidable an adversary"! But when shall we be stronger? Will it be the next week, or the next year? Will it be when we are totally disarmed, and when a British guard shall be stationed in every house? Shall we gather strength by irresolution and inaction? Shall we acquire the means of effectual resistance, by lying supinely on our backs, and hugging the delusive phantom of hope, until our enemies have bound us hand and foot? Sir, we are not weak, if we make a proper use of those means which the God of Nature hath placed in our power. Three millions of people, armed in the holy cause of Liberty, and in such a country as that which we possess, are invincible by any force which our enemy can send against us. Besides, sir, we shall not fight our battles alone. There is a just Power who presides over the destinies of nations, and who will raise up friends to fight our battles for us. The battle, sir, is not to the strong alone; it is to the vigilant, the active, the brave. Besides, sir, we have no election. If we were base enough to desire it, it is now too late to retire from the contest. There is no retreat, but in submission and slavery. Our chains are forged. Their clanking may be heard on the plains of Boston. The war is inevitable; and let it come! I repeat it, sir, let it come! It is in vain, sir, to extenuate the matter. Gentlemen may cry "Peace, peace!" but there is no peace! The war is actually begun! The next gale that sweeps from the north will bring to our ears the clash of resounding arms! Our brethren are already in the field! Why stand we here idle? What is it that gentlemen wish? What would they have? Is life so dear, or peace so sweet, as to be purchased at the price of chains and slavery? Forbid it, Almighty Powers!—I know not what course others may take; but as for me, give me liberty or give me death!

2. Live over in your imagination all the solemnity and sorrow that Lincoln felt at the Gettysburg cemetery. The feeling in this speech is very deep, but it is quieter and more subdued than the preceding one. The purpose of Henry's address was to get action; Lincoln's speech was meant only to dedicate the last resting place of those who had acted. Read it over and over (see page 50) until it burns in your soul. Then commit it and repeat it for emotional expression.

3. Beecher's speech on Lincoln, page 76; Thurston's speech on "A Plea for Cuba," page 50; and the following selection, are recommended for practise in developing feeling in delivery.

A living force that brings to itself all the resources of imagination, all the inspirations of feeling, all that is influential in body, in voice, in eye, in gesture, in posture, in the whole animated man, is in strict analogy with the divine thought and the divine arrangement; and there is no misconstruction more utterly untrue and fatal than this: that oratory is an artificial thing, which deals with baubles and trifles, for the sake of making bubbles of pleasure for transient effect on mercurial audiences. So far from that, it is the consecration of the whole man to the noblest purposes to which one can address himself—the education and inspiration of his fellow men by all that there is in learning, by all that there is in thought, by all that there is in feeling, by all that there is in all of them, sent home through the channels of taste and of beauty.

—HENRY WARD BEECHER.

4. What in your opinion are the relative values of thought and feeling in a speech?

5. Could we dispense with either?

6. What kinds of selections or occasions require much feeling and enthusiasm? Which require little?

7. Invent a list of ten subjects for speeches, saying which would give most room for pure thought and which for feeling.

8. Prepare and deliver a ten–minute speech denouncing the (imaginary) unfeeling plea of an attorney; he may be either the counsel for the defense or the prosecuting attorney, and the accused may be assumed to be either guilty or innocent, at your option.

9. Is feeling more important than the technical principles expounded in chapters III to VII? Why?

10. Analyze the secret of some effective speech or speaker. To what is the success due?

11. Give an example from your own observation of the effect of feeling and enthusiasm on listeners.

12. Memorize Carlyle's and Emerson's remarks on enthusiasm.

13. Deliver Patrick Henry's address, page 110, and Thurston's speech, page 50, without show of feeling or enthusiasm. What is the result?

14. Repeat, with all the feeling these selections demand. What is the result?

15. What steps do you intend to take to develop the power of enthu-

siasm and feeling in speaking?

16. Write and deliver a five–minute speech ridiculing a speaker who uses bombast, pomposity and over–enthusiasm. Imitate him.

11. Fluency Through Preparation

Animis opibusque parati—Ready in mind and resources.

—*Motto of South Carolina.*

In omnibus negotiis prius quam aggrediare, adhibenda est præparatio diligens—In all matters before beginning a diligent preparation should be made.

—CICERO, *De Officiis.*

Take your dictionary and look up the words that contain the Latin stem *flu*—the results will be suggestive.

At first blush it would seem that fluency consists in a ready, easy use of words. Not so—the flowing quality of speech is much more, for it is a composite effect, with each of its prior conditions deserving of careful notice.

The Sources of Fluency

Speaking broadly, fluency is almost entirely a matter of preparation. Certainly, native gifts figure largely here, as in every art, but even natural facility is dependent on the very same laws of preparation that hold good for the man of supposedly small native endowment. Let this encourage you if, like Moses, you are prone to complain that you are not a ready speaker.

Have you ever stopped to analyze that expression, "a ready speaker?" Readiness, in its prime sense, is preparedness, and they are most ready who are best prepared. Quick firing depends more on the alert finger than on the hair trigger. Your fluency will be in direct ratio to two important conditions: your knowledge of what you are going to say, and your being accustomed to telling what you know to an audience. This gives us the second great element of fluency—to preparation must be added the ease that arises from practise; of which more presently.

Knowledge is Essential

Mr. Bryan is a most fluent speaker when he speaks on political problems, tendencies of the time, and questions of morals. It is to be supposed, however, that he would not be so fluent in speaking on the bird life of the Florida Everglades. Mr. John Burroughs might be at his best on this last subject, yet entirely lost in talking about international law. Do not expect to speak fluently on a subject that you know little or nothing about. Ctesiphon boasted that he could speak all day (a sin in itself) on any subject that an audience would suggest. He was banished by the Spartans.

But preparation goes beyond the getting of the facts in the case you are to present: it includes also the ability to think and arrange your thoughts, a full and precise vocabulary, an easy manner of speech and breathing, absence of self–consciousness, and the several other characteristics of efficient delivery that have deserved special attention in other parts of this book rather than in this chapter.

Preparation may be either general or specific; usually it should be both. A life–time of reading, of companionship with stirring thoughts, of wrestling with the problems of life—this constitutes a general preparation of inestimable worth. Out of a well–stored mind, and—richer still—a broad experience, and—best of all—a warmly sympathetic heart, the speaker will have to draw much material that no *immediate* study could provide. General preparation consists of all that a man has put into himself, all that heredity and environment have instilled into him, and—that other rich source of preparedness for speech—the friendship of wise companions. When Schiller returned home after a visit with Goethe a friend remarked: "I am amazed by the progress Schiller can make within a single fortnight." It was the progressive influence of a new friendship. Proper friendships form one of the best means for the formation of ideas and ideals, for they enable one to practise in giving expression to thought. The speaker who would speak fluently before an audience should learn to speak fluently and entertainingly with a friend. Clarify your ideas by putting them in words; the talker gains as much from his conversation as the listener. You sometimes begin to converse on a subject thinking you have very little to say, but one idea gives birth to another, and you are surprised to learn that the more you give the more you have to give. This give–and–take of friendly conversation develops mentality, and fluency in expression. Longfellow said: "A single conversation across the table with a wise man is better than ten years' study of books," and Holmes whimsically yet none the less truthfully declared that half the time he talked to find out what he thought. But that method must not be applied on the platform!

After all this enrichment of life by storage, must come the special preparation for the particular speech. This is of so definite a sort that it warrants separate chapter–treatment later.

Practise

But preparation must also be of another sort than the gathering, organizing, and shaping of materials—it must include *practise*, which, like mental preparation, must be both general and special.

Do not feel surprised or discouraged if practise on the principles of delivery herein laid down seems to retard your fluency. For a time, this will be inevitable. While you are working for proper inflection, for instance, inflection will be demanding your first thoughts, and the flow of your speech, for the time being, will be secondary. This warning, however, is strictly for the closet, for your practise at home. Do not carry any thoughts of inflection with you to the platform. There you must *think* only of your subject. There is an absolute telepathy between the audience and the speaker. If your thought goes to your gesture, their thought will too. If your interest goes to the quality of your voice, they will be regarding that instead of what your voice is uttering.

You have doubtless been adjured to "forget everything but your subject." This advice says either too much or too little. The truth is that while on the platform you must not *forget* a great many things that are not in your subject, but you must not *think* of them. Your attention must consciously go only to your message, but subconsciously you will be attending to the points of technique which have become more or less *habitual by practise.*

A nice balance between these two kinds of attention is important.

You can no more escape this law than you can live without air: Your platform gestures, your voice, your inflection, will all be just as good as your *habit* of gesture, voice, and inflection makes them—no better. Even the thought of whether you are speaking fluently or not will have the effect of marring your flow of speech.

Return to the opening chapter, on self–confidence, and again lay its precepts to heart. Learn by rules to speak without thinking of rules. It is not—or ought not to be—necessary for you to stop to think how to say the alphabet correctly, as a matter of fact it is slightly more difficult for you to repeat Z, Y, X than it is to say X, Y, Z—habit has established the order. Just so you must master the laws of efficiency in speaking until it is a second nature for you to speak correctly rather than otherwise. A beginner at the piano has a great deal of trouble with the mechanics of playing, but as time goes on his fingers become trained and almost instinctively wander over the keys correctly. As an inexperienced speaker you will find a great deal of difficulty at first in putting principles into practise, for you will be scared, like the young swimmer, and make some crude strokes, but if you persevere you will "win out."

Thus, to sum up, the vocabulary you have enlarged by study,[4] the ease in speaking you have developed by practise, the economy of your well–studied emphasis all will subconsciously come to your aid on the platform. Then the habits you have formed will be earning you a splendid dividend. The fluency of your speech will be at the speed of flow your practise has made habitual.

But this means work. What good habit does not? No philosopher's stone that will act as a substitute for laborious practise has ever been found. If it were, it would be thrown away, because it would kill our greatest joy—the delight of acquisition. If public–speaking means to you a fuller life, you will know no greater happiness than a well–spoken speech. The time you have spent in gathering ideas and in private practise of speaking you will find amply rewarded.

QUESTIONS AND EXERCISES

1. What advantages has the fluent speaker over the hesitating talker?

2. What influences, within and without the man himself, work against fluency?

3. Select from the daily paper some topic for an address and make a three–minute address on it. Do your words come freely and your sentences flow out rhythmically? Practise *on the same topic* until they do.

4. Select some subject with which you are familiar and test your fluency by speaking extemporaneously.

5. Take one of the sentiments given below and, following the advice given on pages 118–119, construct a short speech beginning with the last word in the sentence.

Machinery has created a new economic world.

The Socialist Party is a strenuous worker for peace.

He was a crushed and broken man when he left prison.

War must ultimately give way to world–wide arbitration.

The labor unions demand a more equal distribution of the wealth that labor creates.

6. Put the sentiments of Mr. Bryan's "Prince of Peace," on page 448, into your own words. Honestly criticise your own effort.

7. Take any of the following quotations and make a five–minute speech on it without pausing to prepare. The first efforts may be very lame, but if you want speed on a typewriter, a record for a hundred–yard dash, or facility in speaking, you must practise, *practise*, *PRACTISE*.

There lives more faith in honest doubt,
Believe me, than in half the creeds.

—TENNYSON, *In Memoriam.*

Howe'er it be, it seems to me,
'Tis only noble to be good.
Kind hearts are more than coronets,
And simple faith than Norman blood.

—TENNYSON, *Lady Clara Vere de Vere.*

'Tis   distance   lends   enchantment   to   the   view
And robes the mountain in its azure hue.

—CAMPBELL, *Pleasures of Hope.*

His best companions, innocence and health,

And his best riches, ignorance of wealth.

—GOLDSMITH, *The Deserted Village.*

Beware of desperate steps! The darkest day,
Live till tomorrow, will have passed away.

—COWPER, *Needless Alarm.*

My country is the world, and my religion is to do good.

—PAINE, *Rights of Man.*

Trade it may help, society extend,
But lures the pirate, and corrupts the friend:
It raises armies in a nation's aid,
But bribes a senate, and the land's betray'd.

—POPE, *Moral Essays.*[5]

O God, that men should put an enemy in their mouths to steal away
their brains!

—SHAKESPEARE, *Othello.*

It matters not how strait the gate,
How charged with punishment the scroll,
I am the master of my fate,
I am the captain of my soul.

—HENLEY, *Invictus.*

The world is so full of a number of things,
I am sure we should all be happy as kings.

—STEVENSON, *A Child's Garden of Verses.*

If your morals are dreary, depend upon it they are wrong.

—STEVENSON, *Essays.*

Every advantage has its tax. I learn to be content.

—EMERSON, *Essays.*

8. Make a two–minute speech on any of the following general subjects, but you will find that your ideas will come more readily if you narrow your subject by taking some specific phase of it. For instance, instead of trying to speak on "Law" in general, take the proposition, "The Poor Man Cannot Afford to Prosecute;" or instead of dwelling on "Leisure," show how modern speed is creating more leisure. In this way you may expand this subject list indefinitely.

GENERAL THEMES

Law.
Politics.
Woman's Suffrage.
Initiative and Referendum.
A Larger Navy.
War.
Peace.
Foreign Immigration.
The Liquor Traffic.
Labor Unions.
Strikes.
Socialism.
Single Tax.
Tariff.
Honesty.
Courage.
Hope.
Love.
Mercy.
Kindness.
Justice.
Progress.
Machinery.
Invention.
Wealth.
Poverty.
Agriculture.
Science.
Surgery.
Haste.
Leisure.

Happiness.
Health.
Business.
America.
The Far East.
Mobs.
Colleges.
Sports.
Matrimony.
Divorce.
Child Labor.
Education.
Books.
The Theater.
Literature.
Electricity.
Achievement.
Failure.
Public Speaking.
Ideals.
Conversation.
The Most Dramatic Moment of My Life.
My Happiest Days.
Things Worth While.
What I Hope to Achieve.
My Greatest Desire.
What I Would Do with a Million Dollars.
Is Mankind Progressing?
Our Greatest Need.

12. The Voice

Oh, there is something in that voice that reaches
The innermost recesses of my spirit!

—LONGFELLOW, *Christus.*

The dramatic critic of The London *Times* once declared that acting is nine–tenths voice work. Leaving the message aside, the same may justly be said of public speaking. A rich, correctly–used voice is the greatest physical factor of persuasiveness and power, often over–topping the effects of reason.

But a good voice, well handled, is not only an effective possession for the professional speaker, it is a mark of personal culture as well, and even a distinct commercial asset. Gladstone, himself the possessor of a deep, musical voice, has said: "Ninety men in every hundred in the crowded professions will probably never rise above mediocrity because the training of the voice is entirely neglected and considered of no importance." These are words worth pondering.

There are three fundamental requisites for a good voice:

1. Ease

Signor Bonci of the Metropolitan Opera Company says that the secret of good voice is relaxation; and this is true, for relaxation is the basis of ease. The air waves that produce voice result in a different kind of tone when striking against relaxed muscles than when striking constricted muscles. Try this for yourself. Contract the muscles of your face and throat as you do in hate, and flame out "I hate you!" Now relax as you do when thinking gentle, tender thoughts, and say, "I love you." How different the voice sounds.

In practising voice exercises, and in speaking, never force your tones. Ease must be your watchword. The voice is a delicate instrument, and you must not handle it with hammer and tongs. Don't *make* your voice go—*let* it go. Don't work. Let the yoke of speech be easy and its burden light.

Your throat should be free from strain during speech, therefore it is necessary to avoid muscular contraction. The throat must act as a sort of chimney or funnel for the voice, hence any unnatural constriction will not only harm its tones but injure its health.

Nervousness and mental strain are common sources of mouth and throat constriction, so make the battle for poise and self–confidence for which we pleaded in the opening chapter.

But *how* can I relax? you ask. By simply *willing* to relax. Hold your arm out straight from your shoulder. Now—withdraw all power and let it fall. Practise relaxation of the muscles of the throat by letting your neck and head fall forward. Roll the upper part of your body around, with the waist line acting as a pivot. Let your head fall and roll around as you shift the torso to different positions. Do not force your head around—simply relax your neck and let gravity pull it around as your body moves.

Again, let your head fall forward on your breast; raise your head, letting your jaw hang. Relax until your jaw feels heavy, as though it were a weight hung to your face. Remember, you must relax the jaw to obtain command of it. It must be free and flexible for the moulding of tone, and to let the tone pass out unobstructed.

The lips also must be made flexible, to aid in the moulding of clear and beautiful tones. For flexibility of lips repeat the syllables, *mo—me*. In saying *mo*, bring the lips up to resemble the shape of the letter O. In repeating *me* draw them back as you do in a grin. Repeat this exercise rapidly, giving the lips as much exercise as possible.

Try the following exercise in the same manner:

Mo—E—O—E—OO—Ah.

After this exercise has been mastered, the following will also be found excellent for flexibility of lips:

Memorize these *sounds* indicated (not the *expressions*) so that you can repeat them rapidly.

| A as in May. | E as in Met. | U as in Use. | A " Ah. | I " Ice. | Oi " Oil. | A " At. | I " It. | Ou " Our. | O " No. | O " No. | OO " Ooze. | A " All. | OO "

Foot. | A " Ah. | E " Eat. | OO " Ooze. | E " Eat.

All the activity of breathing must be centered, not in the throat, but in the middle of the body—you must breathe from the diaphragm. Note the way you breathe when lying flat on the back, undressed in bed. You will observe that all the activity then centers around the diaphragm. This is the natural and correct method of breathing. By constant watchfulness make this your habitual manner, for it will enable you to relax more perfectly the muscles of the throat.

The next fundamental requisite for good voice is

2. Openness

If the muscles of the throat are constricted, the tone passage partially closed, and the mouth kept half–shut, how can you expect the tone to come out bright and clear, or even to come out at all? Sound is a series of waves, and if you make a prison of your mouth, holding the jaws and lips rigidly, it will be very difficult for the tone to squeeze through, and even when it does escape it will lack force and carrying power. Open your mouth wide, relax all the organs of speech, and let the tone flow out easily.

Start to yawn, but instead of yawning, speak while your throat is open. Make this open–feeling habitual when speaking—we say *make* because it is a matter of resolution and of practise, if your vocal organs are healthy. Your tone passages may be partly closed by enlarged tonsils, adenoids, or enlarged turbinate bones of the nose. If so, a skilled physician should be consulted.

The nose is an important tone passage and should be kept open and free for perfect tones. What we call "talking through the nose" is not talking through the nose, as you can easily demonstrate by holding your nose as you talk. If you are bothered with nasal tones caused by growths or swellings in the nasal passages, a slight, painless operation will remove the obstruction. This is quite important, aside from voice, for the general health will be much lowered if the lungs are continually starved for air.

The final fundamental requisite for good voice is

3. Forwardness

A voice that is pitched back in the throat is dark, sombre, and unattractive. The tone must be pitched forward, but do not *force* it forward. You will recall that our first principle was ease. *Think* the tone forward and out. Believe it is going forward, and allow it to flow easily. You can tell whether you are placing your tone forward or not by inhaling a deep breath and singing *ah* with the mouth wide open, trying to feel the little delicate sound waves strike the bony arch of the mouth just above the front teeth. The sensation is so slight that you will probably not be able to detect it at once, but persevere in your practise, always thinking the tone forward, and you will be rewarded by feeling your voice strike the roof of your mouth. A correct forward–placing of the tone will do away with the dark, throaty tones that are so unpleasant, inefficient, and harmful to the throat.

Close the lips, humming *ng, im,* or *an.* Think the tone forward. Do you feel it strike the lips?

Hold the palm of your hand in front of your face and say vigorously *crash, dash, whirl, buzz.* Can you feel the forward tones strike against your hand? Practise until you can. Remember, the only way to get your voice forward is to *put* it forward.

How to Develop the Carrying Power of the Voice

It is not necessary to speak loudly in order to be heard at a distance. It is necessary only to speak correctly. Edith Wynne Matthison's voice will carry in a whisper throughout a large theater. A paper rustling on the stage of a large auditorium can be heard distinctly in the furthermost seat in the gallery. If you will only use your voice correctly, you will not have much difficulty in being heard. Of course it is always well to address your speech to your furthest auditors; if they get it, those nearer will have no trouble, but aside from this obvious suggestion, you must observe these laws of voice production:

Remember to apply the principles of ease, openness and forwardness—they are the prime factors in enabling your voice to be heard at a distance.

Do not gaze at the floor as you talk. This habit not only gives the speaker an amateurish appearance but if the head is hung forward the voice will be directed towards the ground instead of floating out over the audience.

Voice is a series of air vibrations. To strengthen it two things are necessary: more air or breath, and more vibration.

Breath is the very basis of voice. As a bullet with little powder behind it will not have force and carrying power, so the voice that has little breath behind it will be weak. Not only will deep breathing—breathing from the diaphragm—give the voice a better support, but it will give it a stronger resonance by improving the general health.

Usually, ill health means a weak voice, while abundant physical vitality is shown through a strong, vibrant voice. Therefore anything that improves the general vitality is an excellent voice strengthener, provided you *use* the voice properly. Authorities differ on most of the rules of hygiene but on one point they all agree: vitality and longevity are increased by deep breathing. Practise this until it becomes second nature. Whenever you are speaking, take in deep breaths, but in such a manner that the inhalations will be silent.

Do not try to speak too long without renewing your breath. Nature cares for this pretty well unconsciously in conversation, and she will do the same for you in platform speaking if you do not interfere with her premonitions.

A certain very successful speaker developed voice carrying power by running across country, practising his speeches as he went. The vigorous exercise forced him to take deep breaths, and developed lung power. A hard–fought basketball or tennis game is an efficient way of practising deep breathing. When these methods are not convenient, we recommend the following:

Place your hands at your sides, on the waist line.

By trying to encompass your waist with your fingers and thumbs, force all the air out of the lungs.

Take a deep breath. Remember, all the activity is to be centered in the *middle* of the body; do not raise the shoulders. As the breath is taken your hands will be forced out.

Repeat the exercise, placing your hands on the small of the back and forcing them out as you inhale.

Many methods for deep breathing have been given by various authorities. Get the air into your lungs—that is the important thing.

The body acts as a sounding board for the voice just as the body of the violin acts as a sounding board for its tones. You can increase its vibrations by practise.

Place your finger on your lip and hum the musical scale, thinking and placing the voice forward on the lips. Do you feel the lips vibrate? After a little practise they will vibrate, giving a tickling sensation.

Repeat this exercise, throwing the humming sound into the nose. Hold the upper part of the nose between the thumb and forefinger. Can you feel the nose vibrate?

Placing the palm of your hand on top of your head, repeat this humming exercise. Think the voice there as you hum in head tones. Can you feel the vibration there?

Now place the palm of your hand on the back of your head, repeating the foregoing process. Then try it on the chest. Always remember to think your tone where you desire to feel the vibrations. The mere act of thinking about any portion of your body will tend to make it vibrate.

Repeat the following, after a deep inhalation, endeavoring to feel all portions of your body vibrate at the same time. When you have attained this you will find that it is a pleasant sensation. What ho, my jovial mates. Come on! We will frolic it like fairies, frisking in the merry moonshine.

Purity of Voice

This quality is sometimes destroyed by wasting the breath. Carefully control the breath, using only as much as is necessary for the production of tone. Utilize all that you give out. Failure to do this results in a breathy tone. Take in breath like a prodigal; in speaking, give it out like a miser.

Voice Suggestions

Never attempt to force your voice when hoarse. Do not drink cold water when speaking. The sudden shock to the heated organs of speech will injure the voice. Avoid pitching your voice too high—it will make it raspy. This is a common fault. When you find your voice in too high a range, lower it. Do not wait until you get to the platform to try this. Practise it in your daily conversation. Repeat the alphabet, beginning A on the lowest scale possible and going up a note on each succeeding letter, for the development of range. A wide range will give you facility in making numerous changes of pitch.

Do not form the habit of listening to your voice when speaking. You will need your brain to think of what you are saying—reserve your observation for private practise.

QUESTIONS AND EXERCISES

1. What are the prime requisites for good voice?

2. Tell why each one is necessary for good voice production.

3. Give some exercises for development of these conditions.

4. Why is range of voice desirable?

5. Tell how range of voice may be cultivated.

6. How much daily practise do you consider necessary for the proper development of your voice?

7. How can resonance and carrying power be developed?

8. What are your voice faults?

9. How are you trying to correct them?

13. Voice Charm

A cheerful temper joined with innocence will make beauty attractive, knowledge delightful, and wit good-natured.

—JOSEPH ADDISON, *The Tattler*.

Poe said that "the tone of beauty is sadness," but he was evidently thinking from cause to effect, not contrariwise, for sadness is rarely a producer of beauty—that is peculiarly the province of joy.

The exquisite beauty of a sunset is not exhilarating but tends to a sort of melancholy that is not far from delight The haunting beauty of deep, quiet music holds more than a tinge of sadness. The lovely minor cadences of bird song at twilight are almost depressing.

The reason we are affected to sadness by certain forms of placid beauty is twofold: movement is stimulating and joy-producing, while quietude leads to reflection, and reflection in turn often brings out the tone of regretful longing for that which is past; secondly, quiet beauty produces a vague aspiration for the relatively unattainable, yet does not stimulate to the tremendous effort necessary to make the dimly desired state or object ours.

We must distinguish, for these reasons, between the sadness of beauty and the joy of beauty. True, joy is a deep, inner thing and takes in much more than the idea of bounding, sanguine spirits, for it includes a certain active contentedness of heart. In this chapter, however the word will have its optimistic, exuberant connotation—we are thinking now of vivid, bright-eyed, laughing joy.

Musical, joyous tones constitute voice charm, a subtle magnetism that is delightfully contagious. Now it might seem to the desultory reader that to take the lancet and cut into this alluring voice quality would be to dissect a butterfly wing and so destroy its charm. Yet how can we induce an effect if we are not certain as to the cause?

Nasal Resonance Produces the Bell-tones of the Voice

The tone passages of the nose must be kept entirely free for the bright tones of voice—and after our warning in the preceding chapter you will not confuse what is popularly and erroneously called a "nasal" tone with the true nasal quality, which is so well illustrated by the voice work of trained French singers and speakers.

To develop nasal resonance sing the following, dwelling as long as possible on the *ng* sounds. Pitch the voice in the nasal cavity. Practise both in high and low registers, and develop range—*with brightness.*

Sing–song. Ding–dong. Hong–kong. Long–thong.

Practise in the falsetto voice develops a bright quality in the normal speaking–voice. Try the following, and any other selections you choose, in a falsetto voice. A man's falsetto voice is extremely high and womanish, so men should not practise in falsetto after the exercise becomes tiresome.

She perfectly scorned the best of his clan, and declared the ninth of any man, a perfectly vulgar fraction.

The actress Mary Anderson asked the poet Longfellow what she could do to improve her voice. He replied, "Read aloud daily, joyous, lyric poetry."

The joyous tones are the bright tones. Develop them by exercise. Practise your voice exercises in an attitude of joy. Under the influence of pleasure the body expands, the tone passages open, the action of heart and lungs is accelerated, and all the primary conditions for good tone are established.

More songs float out from the broken windows of the negro cabins in the South than from the palatial homes on Fifth Avenue. Henry Ward Beecher said the happiest days of his life were not when he had become an international character, but when he was an unknown minister out in Lawrenceville, Ohio, sweeping his own church, and working as a carpenter to help pay the grocer. Happiness is largely an attitude of mind, of viewing life from the right angle. The optimistic attitude can be cultivated, and it will express itself in voice charm. A telephone company recently placarded this motto in their booths: "The Voice with the Smile Wins." It does. Try it.

Reading joyous prose, or lyric poetry, will help put smile and joy of soul into your voice. The following selections are excellent for practise.

REMEMBER that when you first practise these classics you are to give sole attention to two things: a joyous attitude of heart and body, and bright tones of voice. After these ends have been attained to your satisfaction, carefully review the principles of public speaking laid down in the preceding chapters and put them into practise as you read these passages again and again. *It would be better to commit each selection to memory.*

SELECTIONS FOR PRACTISE

FROM MILTON'S "L'ALLEGRO"

Haste thee, Nymph, and bring with thee
Jest, and youthful Jollity,
Quips and Cranks and wanton Wiles,
Nods and Becks, and wreathèd Smiles,
Such as hang on Hebe's cheek,
And love to live in dimple sleek,—
Sport that wrinkled Care derides,
And Laughter holding both his sides.

Come, and trip it as ye go
On the light fantastic toe;
And in thy right hand lead with thee
The mountain nymph, sweet Liberty:
And, if I give thee honor due,
Mirth, admit me of thy crew,
To live with her, and live with thee,
In unreprovèd pleasures free;

To hear the lark begin his flight,
And singing, startle the dull Night
From his watch–tower in the skies,
Till the dappled Dawn doth rise;
Then to come in spite of sorrow,
And at my window bid good–morrow
Through the sweetbrier, or the vine,
Or the twisted eglantine;

While the cock with lively din
Scatters the rear of darkness thin,
And to the stack, or the barn–door,
Stoutly struts his dames before;

Oft listening how the hounds and horn
Cheerly rouse the slumbering Morn,
From the side of some hoar hill,
Through the high wood echoing shrill;
Sometime walking, not unseen,
By hedge–row elms, on hillocks green,
Right against the eastern gate,
Where the great Sun begins his state,
Robed in flames and amber light,
The clouds in thousand liveries dight,
While the plowman near at hand
Whistles o'er the furrowed land,
And the milkmaid singing blithe,
And the mower whets his scythe,
And every shepherd tells his tale,
Under the hawthorn in the dale.

THE SEA

The sea, the sea, the open sea,
The blue, the fresh, the fever free;
Without a mark, without a bound,
It runneth the earth's wide regions round;
It plays with the clouds, it mocks the skies,
Or like a cradled creature lies.
I'm on the sea, I'm on the sea,
I am where I would ever be,
With the blue above and the blue below,
And silence wheresoe'er I go.
If a storm should come and awake the deep,
What matter? I shall ride and sleep.

I love, oh! how I love to ride
On the fierce, foaming, bursting tide,
Where every mad wave drowns the moon,
And whistles aloft its tempest tune,

And tells how goeth the world below,
And why the southwest wind doth blow!
I never was on the dull, tame shore

But I loved the great sea more and more,
And backward flew to her billowy breast,
Like a bird that seeketh her mother's nest,—
And a mother she was and is to me,
For I was born on the open sea.

The waves were white, and red the morn,
In the noisy hour when I was born;
The whale it whistled, the porpoise rolled,
And the dolphins bared their backs of gold;
And never was heard such an outcry wild,
As welcomed to life the ocean child.
I have lived, since then, in calm and strife,
Full fifty summers a rover's life,
With wealth to spend, and a power to range,
But never have sought or sighed for change:
And death, whenever he comes to me,
Shall come on the wide, unbounded sea!

—BARRY CORNWALL.

The sun does not shine for a few trees and flowers, but for the wide world's joy. The lonely pine upon the mountain–top waves its sombre boughs, and cries, "Thou art my sun." And the little meadow violet lifts its cup of blue, and whispers with its perfumed breath, "Thou art my sun." And the grain in a thousand fields rustles in the wind, and makes answer, "Thou art my sun." And so God sits effulgent in Heaven, not for a favored few, but for the universe of life; and there is no creature so poor or so low that he may not look up with child–like confidence and say, "My Father! Thou art mine."

—HENRY WARD BEECHER.

THE LARK

Bird of the wilderness,
Blithesome and cumberless,
Sweet be thy matin o'er moorland and lea!

Emblem of happiness,
Blest is thy dwelling–place:
Oh, to abide in the desert with thee!

Wild is thy lay, and loud,
Far in the downy cloud,—
Love gives it energy; love gave it birth.
Where, on thy dewy wing
Where art thou journeying?
Thy lay is in heaven; thy love is on earth.

O'er fell and fountain sheen,
O'er moor and mountain green,
O'er the red streamer that heralds the day;
Over the cloudlet dim,
Over the rainbow's rim,
Musical cherub, soar, singing, away!

Then, when the gloaming comes,
Low in the heather blooms,
Sweet will thy welcome and bed of love be!
Emblem of happiness,
Blest is thy dwelling–place.
Oh, to abide in the desert with thee!

—JAMES HOGG.

In joyous conversation there is an elastic touch, a delicate stroke, upon the central ideas, generally following a pause. This elastic touch adds vivacity to the voice. If you try repeatedly, it can be sensed by feeling the tongue strike the teeth. The entire absence of elastic touch in the voice can be observed in the thick tongue of the intoxicated man. Try to talk with the tongue lying still in the bottom of the mouth, and you will obtain largely the same effect. Vivacity of utterance is gained by using the tongue to strike off the emphatic idea with a decisive, elastic touch.

Deliver the following with decisive strokes on the emphatic ideas. Deliver it in a vivacious manner, noting the elastic touch–action of the tongue. A flexible, responsive tongue is absolutely essential to good voice work.

What have you done with that brilliant France which I left you? I left you at peace, and I find you at war. I left you victorious and I find you defeated. I left you the millions of Italy, and I find only spoliation and poverty. What have you done with the hundred thousand Frenchmen, my companions in glory? They are dead!...This state of affairs cannot last long; in less than three years it would plunge us into despotism.

Practise the following selection, for the development of elastic touch; say it in a joyous spirit, using the exercise to develop voice charm in *all* the ways suggested in this chapter.

THE BROOK

I come from haunts of coot and hern,
I make a sudden sally,
And sparkle out among the fern,
To bicker down a valley.

By thirty hills I hurry down,
Or slip between the ridges;
By twenty thorps, a little town,
And half a hundred bridges.

Till last by Philip's farm I flow
To join the brimming river;
For men may come and men may go,
But I go on forever.

I chatter over stony ways,
In little sharps and trebles,
I bubble into eddying bays,
I babble on the pebbles.

With many a curve my banks I fret,
By many a field and fallow,
And many a fairy foreland set
With willow—weed and mallow.

I chatter, chatter, as I flow

To join the brimming river;
For men may come and men may go,
But I go on forever.

I wind about, and in and out,
With here a blossom sailing,
And here and there a lusty trout,
And here and there a grayling,

And here and there a foamy flake
Upon me, as I travel,
With many a silvery water–break
Above the golden gravel,

And draw them all along, and flow
To join the brimming river,
For men may come and men may go,
But I go on forever.

I steal by lawns and grassy plots,
I slide by hazel covers,
I move the sweet forget–me–nots
That grow for happy lovers.

I slip, I slide, I gloom, I glance,
Among my skimming swallows;
I make the netted sunbeam dance
Against my sandy shallows,

I murmur under moon and stars
In brambly wildernesses,
I linger by my shingly bars,
I loiter round my cresses;

And out again I curve and flow
To join the brimming river;
For men may come and men may go,
But I go on forever.

—ALFRED TENNYSON.

The children at play on the street, glad from sheer physical vitality, display a resonance and charm in their voices quite different from the voices that float through the silent halls of the hospitals.

A skilled physician can tell much about his patient's condition from the mere sound of the voice. Failing health, or even physical weariness, tells through the voice. It is always well to rest and be entirely refreshed before attempting to deliver a public address. As to health, neither scope nor space permits us to discuss here the laws of hygiene. There are many excellent books on this subject. In the reign of the Roman emperor Tiberius, one senator wrote to another: "To the wise, a word is sufficient."

"The apparel oft proclaims the man;" the voice always does—it is one of the greatest revealers of character. The superficial woman, the brutish man, the reprobate, the person of culture, often discloses inner nature in the voice, for even the cleverest dissembler cannot entirely prevent its tones and qualities being affected by the slightest change of thought or emotion. In anger it becomes high, harsh, and unpleasant; in love low, soft, and melodious—the variations are as limitless as they are fascinating to observe.

Visit a theatrical hotel in a large city, and listen to the buzz–saw voices of the chorus girls from some burlesque "attraction." The explanation is simple—buzz–saw lives. Emerson said: "When a man lives with God his voice shall be as sweet as the murmur of the brook or the rustle of the corn." It is impossible to think selfish thoughts and have either an attractive personality, a lovely character, or a charming voice. If you want to possess voice charm, cultivate a deep, sincere sympathy for mankind. Love will shine out through your eyes and proclaim itself in your tones. One secret of the sweetness of the canary's song may be his freedom from tainted thoughts. Your character beautifies or mars your voice. As a man thinketh in his heart so is his voice.

QUESTIONS AND EXERCISES

1. Define (*a*) charm; (*b*) joy; (*c*) beauty.

2. Make a list of all the words related to *joy*.

3. Write a three–minute eulogy of "The Joyful Man."

4. Deliver it without the use of notes. Have you carefully considered all

the qualities that go to make up voice–charm in its delivery?

5. Tell briefly in your own words what means may be employed to develop a charming voice.

6. Discuss the effect of voice on character.

7. Discuss the effect of character on voice.

8. Analyze the voice charm of any speaker or singer you choose.

9. Analyze the defects of any given voice.

10. Make a short humorous speech imitating certain voice defects, pointing out reasons.

11. Commit the following stanza and interpret each phase of delight suggested or expressed by the poet.

An infant when it gazes on a light,
A child the moment when it drains the breast,
A devotee when soars the Host in sight,
An Arab with a stranger for a guest,
A sailor when the prize has struck in fight,
A miser filling his most hoarded chest,
Feel rapture; but not such true joy are reaping
As they who watch o'er what they love while sleeping.

—BYRON, *Don Juan.*

14. Distinctness And Precision Of Utterance

In man speaks God.

—HESIOD, *Words and Days.*

And endless are the modes of speech, and far
Extends from side to side the field of words.

—HOMER, *Iliad.*

In popular usage the terms "pronunciation," "enunciation," and "artic-
ulation" are synonymous, but real pronunciation includes three dis-
tinct processes, and may therefore be defined as, *the utterance of a
syllable or a group of syllables with regard to articulation, accentuation,
and enunciation.*

Distinct and precise utterance is one of the most important consider-
ations of public speech. How preposterous it is to hear a speaker mak-
ing sounds of "inarticulate earnestness" under the contented delusion
that he is telling something to his audience! Telling? Telling means
communicating, and how can he actually communicate without mak-
ing every word distinct?

Slovenly pronunciation results from either physical deformity or habit.
A surgeon or a surgeon dentist may correct a deformity, but your own
will, working by self–observation and resolution in drill, will break a
habit. All depends upon whether you think it worth while.

Defective speech is so widespread that freedom from it is the excep-
tion. It is painfully common to hear public speakers mutilate the king's
English. If they do not actually murder it, as Curran once said, they
often knock an *i* out.

A Canadian clergyman, writing in the *Homiletic Review*, relates that in his student days "a classmate who was an Englishman supplied a country church for a Sunday. On the following Monday he conducted a missionary meeting. In the course of his address he said some farmers thought they were doing their duty toward missions when they gave their 'hodds and hends' to the work, but the Lord required more. At the close of the meeting a young woman seriously said to a friend: 'I am sure the farmers do well if they give their hogs and hens to missions. It is more than most people can afford.'"

It is insufferable effrontery for any man to appear before an audience who persists in driving the *h* out of happiness, home and heaven, and, to paraphrase Waldo Messaros, will not let it rest in hell. He who does not show enough self–knowledge to see in himself such glaring faults, nor enough self–mastery to correct them, has no business to instruct others. If he *can* do no better, he should be silent. If he *will* do no better, he should also be silent.

Barring incurable physical defects—and few are incurable nowadays— the whole matter is one of will. The catalogue of those who have done the impossible by faithful work is as inspiring as a roll–call of warriors. "The less there is of you," says Nathan Sheppard, "the more need for you to make the most of what there is of you."

Articulation

Articulation is the forming and joining of the elementary sounds of speech. It seems an appalling task to utter articulately the third–of–a million words that go to make up our English vocabulary, but the way to make a beginning is really simple: *learn to utter correctly, and with easy change from one to the other, each of the forty–four elementary sounds in our language.*

The reasons why articulation is so painfully slurred by a great many public speakers are four: ignorance of the elemental sounds; failure to discriminate between sounds nearly alike; a slovenly, lazy use of the vocal organs; and a torpid will. Anyone who is still master of himself will know how to handle each of these defects.

The vowel sounds are the most vexing source of errors, especially where diphthongs are found. Who has not heard such errors as are hit off in this inimitable verse by Oliver Wendell Holmes:

Learning condemns beyond the reach of hope
The careless lips that speak of sŏap for sōap;
Her edict exiles from her fair abode
The clownish voice that utters rŏad for rōad;
Less stern to him who calls his cōat, a coat
And steers his bōat believing it a bŏat.
She pardoned one, our classic city's boast.
Who said at Cambridge, mŏst instead of mōst,
But knit her brows and stamped her angry foot
To hear a Teacher call a rōōt a rŏŏt.

The foregoing examples are all monosyllables, but bad articulation is frequently the result of joining sounds that do not belong together. For example, no one finds it difficult to say *beauty*, but many persist in pronouncing *duty* as though it were spelled either *dooty* or *juty*. It is not only from untaught speakers that we hear such slovenly articulations as *colyum* for *column*, and *pritty* for *pretty*, but even great orators occasionally offend quite as unblushingly as less noted mortals.

Nearly all such are errors of carelessness, not of pure ignorance—of carelessness because the ear never tries to hear what the lips articulate. It must be exasperating to a foreigner to find that the elemental sound *ou* gives him no hint for the pronunciation of *bough, cough, rough, thorough,* and *through,* and we can well forgive even a man of culture who occasionally loses his way amidst the intricacies of English articulation, but there can be no excuse for the slovenly utterance of the simple vowel sounds which form at once the life and the beauty of our language. He who is too lazy to speak distinctly should hold his tongue.

The consonant sounds occasion serious trouble only for those who do not look with care at the spelling of words about to be pronounced. Nothing but carelessness can account for saying *Jacop, Babtist, sevem, alwus,* or *sadisfy.*

"He that hath yaws to yaw, let him yaw," is the rendering which an Anglophobiac clergyman gave of the familiar scripture, "He that hath ears to hear, let him hear." After hearing the name of Sir Humphry Davy pronounced, a Frenchman who wished to write to the eminent

Englishman thus addressed the letter: "Serum Fridavi."

Accentuation

Accentuation is the stressing of the proper syllables in words. This it is that is popularly called *pronunciation*. For instance, we properly say that a word is mispronounced when it is accented *in'–vite* instead of *in–vite'*, though it is really an offense against only one form of pronunciation—accentuation.

It is the work of a lifetime to learn the accents of a large vocabulary and to keep pace with changing usage; but an alert ear, the study of word–origins, and the dictionary habit, will prove to be mighty helpers in a task that can never be finally completed.

Enunciation

Correct enunciation is the complete utterance of all the sounds of a syllable or a word. Wrong articulation gives the wrong sound to the vowel or vowels of a word or a syllable, as *doo* for *dew;* or unites two sounds improperly, as *hully* for *wholly*. Wrong enunciation is the *incomplete* utterance of a syllable or a word, the sound omitted or added being usually consonantal. To say *needcessity* instead of *necessity* is a wrong articulation; to say *doin* for *doing* is improper enunciation. The one articulates—that is, joints—two sounds that should not be joined, and thus gives the word a positively wrong sound; the other fails to touch all the sounds in the word, and *in that particular way* also sounds the word incorrectly.

"My tex' may be foun' in the fif' and six' verses of the secon' chapter of Titus; and the subjec' of my discourse is 'The Gover'ment of ar Homes.'"

What did this preacher do with his final consonants? This slovenly dropping of essential sounds is as offensive as the common habit of running words together so that they lose their individuality and distinctness. *Lighten dark, uppen down, doncher know, partic'lar, zamination*, are all too common to need comment.

Imperfect enunciation is due to lack of attention and to lazy lips. It can be corrected by resolutely attending to the formation of syllables as they are uttered. Flexible lips will enunciate difficult combinations of sounds without slighting any of them, but such flexibility cannot be attained except by habitually uttering words with distinctness and accuracy. A daily exercise in enunciating a series of sounds will in a short time give flexibility to the lips and alertness to the mind, so that no word will be uttered without receiving its due complement of sound.

Returning to our definition, we see that when the sounds of a word are properly articulated, the right syllables accented, and full value given to each sound in its enunciation, we have correct pronunciation. Perhaps one word of caution is needed here, lest any one, anxious to bring out clearly every sound, should overdo the matter and neglect the unity and smoothness of pronunciation. Be careful not to bring syllables into so much prominence as to make words seem long and angular. The joints must be kept decently dressed.

Before delivery, do not fail to go over your manuscript and note every sound that may possibly be mispronounced. Consult the dictionary and make assurance doubly sure. If the arrangement of words is unfavorable to clear enunciation, change either words or order and do not rest until you can follow Hamlet's directions to the players.

QUESTIONS AND EXERCISES

1. Practise repeating the following rapidly, paying particular attention to the consonants.

"Foolish Flavius, flushing feverishly, fiercely found fault with Flora's frivolity."

Mary's matchless mimicry makes much mischief.

Seated on shining shale she sells sea shells.

You youngsters yielded your youthful yule–tide yearnings yesterday.

2. Sound the *l* in each of the following words, repeated in sequence:

Blue black blinkers blocked Black Blondin's eyes.

3. Do you say a *bloo* sky or a *blue* sky?

4. Compare the *u* sound in *few* and in *new*. Say each aloud, and decide which is correct, *Noo York*, *New Yawk*, or *New York*?

5. Pay careful heed to the directions of this chapter in reading the following, from Hamlet. After the interview with the ghost of his father, Hamlet tells his friends Horatio and Marcellus that he intends to act a part:

Horatio. O day and night, but this is wondrous strange!

Hamlet. And therefore as a stranger give it welcome.

There are more things in heaven and earth, Horatio,

Than are dreamt of in your philosophy.

But come;

Here, as before, never, so help you mercy,

How strange or odd so'er I bear myself,—

As I perchance hereafter shall think meet

To put an antic disposition on,—

That you, at such times seeing me, never shall,

With arms encumber'd thus, or this head–shake,

Or by pronouncing of some doubtful phrase,

As "Well, well, we know," or "We could, an if we would,"

Or "If we list to speak," or "There be, an if there might,"

Or such ambiguous giving–out, to note

That you know aught of me: this not to do,

So grace and mercy at your most need help you,

Swear.

—Act I. Scene V.

6. Make a list of common errors of pronunciation, saying which are due to faulty articulation, wrong accentuation, and incomplete enun-

ciation. In each case make the correction.

7. Criticise any speech you may have heard which displayed these faults.

8. Explain how the false shame of seeming to be too precise may hinder us from cultivating perfect verbal utterance.

9. Over–precision is likewise a fault. To bring out any syllable unduly is to caricature the word. Be *moderate* in reading the following:

THE LAST SPEECH OF MAXIMILIAN DE ROBESPIERRE

The enemies of the Republic call me tyrant! Were I such they would grovel at my feet. I should gorge them with gold, I should grant them immunity for their crimes, and they would be grateful. Were I such, the kings we have vanquished, far from denouncing Robespierre, would lend me their guilty support; there would be a covenant between them and me. Tyranny must have tools. But the enemies of tyranny,—whither does their path tend? To the tomb, and to immortality! What tyrant is my protector? To what faction do I belong? Yourselves! What faction, since the beginning of the Revolution, has crushed and annihilated so many detected traitors? You, the people,—our principles—are that faction—a faction to which I am devoted, and against which all the scoundrelism of the day is banded!

The confirmation of the Republic has been my object; and I know that the Republic can be established only on the eternal basis of morality. Against me, and against those who hold kindred principles, the league is formed. My life? Oh! my life I abandon without a regret! I have seen the past; and I foresee the future. What friend of this country would wish to survive the moment when he could no longer serve it,—when he could no longer defend innocence against oppression? Wherefore should I continue in an order of things, where intrigue eternally triumphs over truth; where justice is mocked; where passions the most abject, or fears the most absurd, over–ride the sacred interests of humanity? In witnessing the multitude of vices which the torrent of the Revolution has rolled in turbid communion with its civic virtues, I confess that I have sometimes feared that I should be sullied, in the eyes of posterity, by the impure neighborhood of unprincipled men, who had thrust themselves into association with the sincere friends of humanity; and I rejoice that these conspirators against my country have now, by their reckless rage, traced deep the line of demarcation between themselves and all true men.

Question history, and learn how all the defenders of liberty, in all times, have been overwhelmed by calumny. But their traducers died also. The good and the bad disappear alike from the earth; but in very different conditions. O Frenchmen! O my countrymen! Let not your enemies, with their desolating doctrines, degrade your souls, and enervate your virtues! No, Chaumette, no! Death is not "an eternal sleep!" Citizens! efface from the tomb that motto, graven by sacrilegious hands, which spreads over all nature a funereal crape, takes from oppressed innocence its support, and affronts the beneficent dispensation of death! Inscribe rather thereon these words: "Death is the commencement of immortality!" I leave to the oppressors of the People a terrible testament, which I proclaim with the independence befitting one whose career is so nearly ended; it is the awful truth - "Thou shalt die!"

15. The Truth About Gesture

When Whitefield acted an old blind man advancing by slow steps toward the edge of the precipice, Lord Chesterfield started up and cried: "Good God, he is gone!"

—NATHAN SHEPPARD, *Before an Audience.*

Gesture is really a simple matter that requires observation and common sense rather than a book of rules. Gesture is an outward expression of an inward condition. It is merely an effect—the effect of a mental or an emotional impulse struggling for expression through physical avenues.

You must not, however, begin at the wrong end: if you are troubled by your gestures, or a lack of gestures, attend to the cause, not the effect. It will not in the least help matters to tack on to your delivery a few mechanical movements. If the tree in your front yard is not growing to suit you, fertilize and water the soil and let the tree have sunshine. Obviously it will not help your tree to nail on a few branches. If your cistern is dry, wait until it rains; or bore a well. Why plunge a pump into a dry hole?

The speaker whose thoughts and emotions are welling within him like a mountain spring will not have much trouble to make gestures; it will be merely a question of properly directing them. If his enthusiasm for his subject is not such as to give him a natural impulse for dramatic action, it will avail nothing to furnish him with a long list of rules. He may tack on some movements, but they will look like the wilted branches nailed to a tree to simulate life. Gestures must be born, not built. A wooden horse may amuse the children, but it takes a live one to go somewhere.

It is not only impossible to lay down definite rules on this subject, but it would be silly to try, for everything depends on the speech, the occasion, the personality and feelings of the speaker, and the attitude of the audience. It is easy enough to forecast the result of multiplying seven by six, but it is impossible to tell any man what kind of gestures he will be impelled to use when he wishes to show his earnestness. We may tell him that many speakers close the hand, with the exception of the forefinger, and pointing that finger straight at the audience pour out their thoughts like a volley; or that others stamp one foot for emphasis; or that Mr. Bryan often slaps his hands together for great force, holding one palm upward in an easy manner; or that Gladstone would sometimes make a rush at the clerk's table in Parliament and smite it with his hand so forcefully that D'israeli once brought down the house by grimly congratulating himself that such a barrier stood between himself and "the honorable gentleman."

All these things, and a bookful more, may we tell the speaker, but we cannot know whether he can use these gestures or not, any more than we can decide whether he could wear Mr. Bryan's clothes. The best that can be done on this subject is to offer a few practical suggestions, and let personal good taste decide as to where effective dramatic action ends and extravagant motion begins.

Any Gesture That Merely Calls Attention to Itself Is Bad

The purpose of a gesture is to carry your thought and feeling into the minds and hearts of your hearers; this it does by emphasizing your message, by interpreting it, by expressing it in action, by striking its tone in either a physically descriptive, a suggestive, or a typical gesture—and let it be remembered all the time that gesture includes *all* physical movement, from facial expression and the tossing of the head to the expressive movements of hand and foot. A shifting of the pose may be a most effective gesture.

What is true of gesture is true of all life. If the people on the street turn around and watch your walk, your walk is more important than you are—change it. If the attention of your audience is called to your gestures, they are not convincing, because they *appear* to be—what they have a doubtful right to be in reality—studied. Have you ever seen a speaker use such grotesque gesticulations that you were fascinated by their frenzy of oddity, but could not follow his thought? Do not smother ideas with gymnastics. Savonarola would rush down from the high pulpit among the congregation in the *duomo* at Florence and carry the fire of conviction to his hearers; Billy Sunday slides to base on the platform carpet in dramatizing one of his baseball illustrations. Yet in both instances the message has somehow stood out bigger than the gesture—it is chiefly in calm afterthought that men have remembered the *form* of dramatic expression. When Sir Henry Irving made his famous exit as "Shylock" the last thing the audience saw was his pallid, avaricious hand extended skinny and claw–like against the background. At the time, every one was overwhelmed by the tremendous typical quality of this gesture; now, we have time to think of its art, and discuss its realistic power.

Only when gesture is subordinated to the absorbing importance of the idea—a spontaneous, living expression of living truth—is it justifiable at all; and when it is remembered for itself—as a piece of unusual physical energy or as a poem of grace—it is a dead failure as dramatic expression. There is a place for a unique style of walking—it is the circus or the cake–walk; there is a place for surprisingly rhythmical evolutions of arms and legs—it is on the dance floor or the stage. Don't let your agility and grace put your thoughts out of business.

One of the present writers took his first lessons in gesture from a certain college president who knew far more about what had happened at the Diet of Worms than he did about how to express himself in action. His instructions were to start the movement on a certain word, continue it on a precise curve, and unfold the fingers at the conclusion, ending with the forefinger—just so. Plenty, and more than plenty, has been published on this subject, giving just such silly directions. Gesture is a thing of mentality and feeling—not a matter of geometry. Remember, whenever a pair of shoes, a method of pronunciation, or a gesture calls attention to itself, it is bad. When you have made really good gestures in a good speech your hearers will not go away saying, "What beautiful gestures he made!" but they will say, "I'll vote for that measure." "He is right—I believe in that."

Gestures Should Be Born of the Moment

The best actors and public speakers rarely know in advance what gestures they are going to make. They make one gesture on certain words tonight, and none at all tomorrow night at the same point— their various moods and interpretations govern their gestures. It is all a matter of impulse and intelligent feeling with them—don't overlook that word *intelligent*. Nature does not always provide the same kind of sunsets or snow flakes, and the movements of a good speaker vary almost as much as the creations of nature.

Now all this is not to say that you must not take some thought for your gestures. If that were meant, why this chapter? When the sergeant despairingly besought the recruit in the awkward squad to step out and look at himself, he gave splendid advice—and worthy of personal application. Particularly while you are in the learning days of public speaking you must learn to criticise your own gestures. Recall them— see where they were useless, crude, awkward, what not, and do better next time. There is a vast deal of difference between being conscious of self and being self–conscious.

It will require your nice discrimination in order to cultivate sponta- neous gestures and yet give due attention to practise. While you de- pend upon the moment it is vital to remember that only a dramatic genius can effectively accomplish such feats as we have related of Whitefield, Savonarola, and others: and doubtless the first time they were used they came in a burst of spontaneous feeling, yet Whitefield declared that not until he had delivered a sermon forty times was its delivery perfected. What spontaneity initiates let practise complete. Every effective speaker and every vivid actor has observed, considered and practised gesture until his dramatic actions are a sub–conscious possession, just like his ability to pronounce correctly without especial- ly concentrating his thought. Every able platform man has possessed himself of a dozen ways in which he might depict in gesture any given emotion; in fact, the means for such expression are endless—and this is precisely why it is both useless and harmful to make a chart of ges- tures and enforce them as the ideals of what may be used to express this or that feeling. Practise descriptive, suggestive, and typical move- ments until they come as naturally as a good articulation; and rarely forecast the gestures you will use at a given moment: leave something to that moment.

Avoid Monotony in Gesture

Roast beef is an excellent dish, but it would be terrible as an exclusive diet. No matter how effective one gesture is, do not overwork it. Put variety in your actions. Monotony will destroy all beauty and power. The pump handle makes one effective gesture, and on hot days that one is very eloquent, but it has its limitations.

Any Movement that is not Significant, Weakens

Do not forget that. Restlessness is not expression. A great many useless movements will only take the attention of the audience from what you are saying. A widely-noted man introduced the speaker of the evening one Sunday lately to a New York audience. The only thing remembered about that introductory speech is that the speaker played nervously with the covering of the table as he talked. We naturally watch moving objects. A janitor putting down a window can take the attention of the hearers from Mr. Roosevelt. By making a few movements at one side of the stage a chorus girl may draw the interest of the spectators from a big scene between the "leads." When our forefathers lived in caves they had to watch moving objects, for movements meant danger. We have not yet overcome the habit. Advertisers have taken advantage of it—witness the moving electric light signs in any city. A shrewd speaker will respect this law and conserve the attention of his audience by eliminating all unnecessary movements.

Gesture Should either be Simultaneous with or Precede the Words—not Follow Them

Lady Macbeth says: "Bear welcome in your eye, your hand, your tongue." Reverse this order and you get comedy. Say, "There he goes," pointing at him after you have finished your words, and see if the result is not comical.

Do Not Make Short, Jerky Movements

Some speakers seem to be imitating a waiter who has failed to get a tip. Let your movements be easy, and from the shoulder, as a rule, rather than from the elbow. But do not go to the other extreme and make too many flowing motions—that savors of the lackadaisical.

Put a little "punch" and life into your gestures. You can not, however, do this mechanically. The audience will detect it if you do. They may not know just what is wrong, but the gesture will have a false appearance to them.

Facial Expression is Important

Have you ever stopped in front of a Broadway theater and looked at the photographs of the cast? Notice the row of chorus girls who are supposed to be expressing fear. Their attitudes are so mechanical that the attempt is ridiculous. Notice the picture of the "star" expressing the same emotion: his muscles are drawn, his eyebrows lifted, he shrinks, and fear shines through his eyes. That actor *felt* fear when the photograph was taken. The chorus girls felt that it was time for a rarebit, and more nearly expressed that emotion than they did fear. Incidentally, that is one reason why they *stay* in the chorus.

The movements of the facial muscles may mean a great deal more than the movements of the hand. The man who sits in a dejected heap with a look of despair on his face is expressing his thoughts and feelings just as effectively as the man who is waving his arms and shouting from the back of a dray wagon. The eye has been called the window of the soul. Through it shines the light of our thoughts and feelings.

Do Not Use Too Much Gesture

As a matter of fact, in the big crises of life we do not go through many actions. When your closest friend dies you do not throw up your hands and talk about your grief. You are more likely to sit and brood in dry–eyed silence. The Hudson River does not make much noise on its way to the sea—it is not half so loud as the little creek up in Bronx Park that a bullfrog could leap across. The barking dog never tears your trousers—at least they say he doesn't. Do not fear the man who waves his arms and shouts his anger, but the man who comes up quietly with eyes flaming and face burning may knock you down. Fuss is not force. Observe these principles in nature and practise them in your delivery.

The writer of this chapter once observed an instructor drilling a class in gesture. They had come to the passage from Henry VIII in which the humbled Cardinal says: "Farewell, a long farewell to all my greatness." It is one of the pathetic passages of literature. A man uttering such a sentiment would be crushed, and the last thing on earth he would do would be to make flamboyant movements. Yet this class had an elocutionary manual before them that gave an appropriate gesture for every occasion, from paying the gas bill to death–bed farewells. So they were instructed to throw their arms out at full length on each side and say: "Farewell, a long farewell to all my greatness." Such a gesture might possibly be used in an after–dinner speech at the convention of a telephone company whose lines extended from the Atlantic to the Pacific, but to think of Wolsey's using that movement would suggest that his fate was just.

Posture

The physical attitude to be taken before the audience really is included in gesture. Just what that attitude should be depends, not on rules, but on the spirit of the speech and the occasion. Senator La Follette stood for three hours with his weight thrown on his forward foot as he leaned out over the footlights, ran his fingers through his hair, and flamed out a denunciation of the trusts. It was very effective. But imagine a speaker taking that kind of position to discourse on the development of road–making machinery. If you have a fiery, aggressive message, and will let yourself go, nature will naturally pull your weight to your forward foot. A man in a hot political argument or a street brawl never has to stop to think upon which foot he should throw his weight. You may sometimes place your weight on your back foot if you have a restful and calm message—but don't worry about it: just stand like a man who genuinely feels what he is saying. Do not stand with your heels close together, like a soldier or a butler. No more should you stand with them wide apart like a traffic policeman. Use simple good manners and common sense.

Here a word of caution is needed. We have advised you to allow your gestures and postures to be spontaneous and not woodenly prepared beforehand, but do not go to the extreme of ignoring the importance of acquiring mastery of your physical movements. A muscular hand made flexible by free movement, is far more likely to be an effective instrument in gesture than a stiff, pudgy bunch of fingers. If your shoulders are lithe and carried well, while your chest does not retreat from association with your chin, the chances of using good extemporaneous gestures are so much the better. Learn to keep the *back* of your neck touching your collar, hold your chest high, and keep down your waist measure.

So attention to strength, poise, flexibility, and grace of body are the foundations of good gesture, for they are expressions of vitality, and without vitality no speaker can enter the kingdom of power. When an awkward giant like Abraham Lincoln rose to the sublimest heights of oratory he did so because of the greatness of his soul—his very ruggedness of spirit and artless honesty were properly expressed in his gnarly body. The fire of character, of earnestness, and of message swept his hearers before him when the tepid words of an insincere Apollo would have left no effect. But be sure you are a second Lincoln before you despise the handicap of physical awkwardness.

"Ty" Cobb has confided to the public that when he is in a batting slump he even stands before a mirror, bat in hand, to observe the "swing" and "follow through" of his batting form. If you would learn to stand well before an audience, look at yourself in a mirror—but not too often. Practise walking and standing before the mirror so as to conquer awkwardness—not to cultivate a pose. Stand on the platform in the same easy manner that you would use before guests in a drawing–room. If your position is not graceful, make it so by dancing, gymnasium work, and *by getting grace and poise in your mind*.

Do not continually hold the same position. Any big change of thought necessitates a change of position. Be at home. There are no rules—it is all a matter of taste. While on the platform forget that you have any hands until you desire to use them—then remember them effectively. Gravity will take care of them. Of course, if you want to put them behind you, or fold them once in awhile, it is not going to ruin your speech. Thought and feeling are the big things in speaking—not the position of a foot or a hand. Simply *put* your limbs where you want them to be—you have a will, so do not neglect to use it.

Let us reiterate, do not despise practise. Your gestures and movements may be spontaneous and still be wrong. No matter how natural they are, it is possible to improve them.

It is impossible for anyone—even yourself—to criticise your gestures until after they are made. You can't prune a peach tree until it comes up; therefore speak much, and observe your own speech. While you are examining yourself, do not forget to study statuary and paintings to see how the great portrayers of nature have made their subjects express ideas through action. Notice the gestures of the best speakers and actors. Observe the physical expression of life everywhere. The leaves on the tree respond to the slightest breeze. The muscles of your face, the light of your eyes, should respond to the slightest change of feeling. Emerson says: "Every man that I meet is my superior in some way. In that I learn of him." Illiterate Italians make gestures so wonderful and beautiful that Booth or Barrett might have sat at their feet and been instructed. Open your eyes. Emerson says again: "We are immersed in beauty, but our eyes have no clear vision." Toss this book to one side; go out and watch one child plead with another for a bite of apple; see a street brawl; observe life in action. Do you want to know how to express victory? Watch the victors' hands go high on election night. Do you want to plead a cause? Make a composite photograph of all the pleaders in daily life you constantly see. Beg, borrow, and steal the best you can get, *BUT DON'T GIVE IT OUT AS THEFT.* Assimilate it until it becomes a part of you—then *let* the expression come out.

QUESTIONS AND EXERCISES

1. From what source do you intend to study gesture?

2. What is the first requisite of good gestures? Why?

3. Why is it impossible to lay down steel–clad rules for gesturing?

4. Describe (*a*) a graceful gesture that you have observed; (*b*) a forceful one; (*c*) an extravagant one; (*d*) an inappropriate one.

5. What gestures do you use for emphasis? Why?

6. How can grace of movement be acquired?

7. When in doubt about a gesture what would you do?

8. What, according to your observations before a mirror, are your faults in gesturing?

9. How do you intend to correct them?

10. What are some of the gestures, if any, that you might use in delivering Thurston's speech, page 50; Grady's speech, page 36? Be specific.

11. Describe some particularly appropriate gesture that you have observed. Why was it appropriate?

12. Cite at least three movements in nature that might well be imitated in gesture.

13. What would you gather from the expressions: *descriptive* gesture, *suggestive* gesture, and *typical* gesture?

14. Select any elemental emotion, such as fear, and try, by picturing in your mind at least five different situations that might call forth this

emotion, to express its several phases by gesture—including posture, movement, and facial expression.

15. Do the same thing for such other emotions as you may select.

16. Select three passages from any source, only being sure that they are suitable for public delivery, memorize each, and then devise gestures suitable for each. Say why.

17. Criticise the gestures in any speech you have heard recently.

18. Practise flexible movement of the hand. What exercises did you find useful?

19. Carefully observe some animal; then devise several typical gestures.

20. Write a brief dialogue between any two animals; read it aloud and invent expressive gestures.

21. Deliver, with appropriate gestures, the quotation that heads this chapter.

22. Read aloud the following incident, using dramatic gestures:

When Voltaire was preparing a young actress to appear in one of his tragedies, he tied her hands to her sides with pack thread in order to check her tendency toward exuberant gesticulation. Under this condition of compulsory immobility she commenced to rehearse, and for some time she bore herself calmly enough; but at last, completely carried away by her feelings, she burst her bonds and flung up her arms. Alarmed at her supposed neglect of his instructions, she began to apologize to the poet; he smilingly reassured her, however; the gesture was *then* admirable, because it was irrepressible.

—REDWAY, *The Actor's Art.*

23. Render the following with suitable gestures:

One day, while preaching, Whitefield "suddenly assumed a nautical air and manner that were irresistible with him," and broke forth in these words: "Well, my boys, we have a clear sky, and are making fine headway over a smooth sea before a light breeze, and we shall soon lose sight of land. But what means this sudden lowering of the heavens, and that dark cloud arising from beneath the western horizon? Hark! Don't you hear distant thunder? Don't you see those flashes of lightning? There is a storm gathering! Every man to his duty! The air is dark!—the tempest rages!—our masts are gone!—the ship is on her beam ends! What next?" At this a number of sailors in the congregation, utterly swept away by the dramatic description, leaped to their feet and cried: "The longboat!—take to the longboat!"

—NATHAN SHEPPARD, *Before an Audience.*

16. Methods Of Delivery

The crown, the consummation, of the discourse is its delivery. Toward it all preparation looks, for it the audience waits, by it the speaker is judged.... All the forces of the orator's life converge in his oratory. The logical acuteness with which he marshals the facts around his theme, the rhetorical facility with which he orders his language, the control to which he has attained in the use of his body as a single organ of expression, whatever richness of acquisition and experience are his—these all are now incidents; *the fact* is the sending of his message home to his hearers.... The hour of delivery is the "supreme, inevitable hour" for the orator. It is this fact that makes lack of adequate preparation such an impertinence. And it is this that sends such thrills of indescribable joy through the orator's whole being when he has achieved a success—it is like the mother forgetting her pangs for the joy of bringing a son into the world.

—J.B.E., *How to Attract and Hold an Audience.*

There are four fundamental methods of delivering an address; all others are modifications of one or more of these: reading from manuscript, committing the written speech and speaking from memory, speaking from notes, and extemporaneous speech. It is impossible to say which form of delivery is best for all speakers in all circumstances—in deciding for yourself you should consider the occasion, the nature of the audience, the character of your subject, and your own limitations of time and ability. However, it is worth while warning you not to be lenient in self-exaction. Say to yourself courageously: What others can do, I can attempt. A bold spirit conquers where others flinch, and a trying task challenges pluck.

Reading from Manuscript

This method really deserves short shrift in a book on public speaking, for, delude yourself as you may, public reading is not public speaking. Yet there are so many who grasp this broken reed for support that we must here discuss the "read speech"—apologetic misnomer as it is.

Certainly there are occasions—among them, the opening of Congress, the presentation of a sore question before a deliberative body, or a historical commemoration—when it may seem not alone to the "orator" but to all those interested that the chief thing is to express certain thoughts in precise language—in language that *must* not be either misunderstood or misquoted. At such times oratory is unhappily elbowed to a back bench, the manuscript is solemnly withdrawn from the capacious inner pocket of the new frock coat, and everyone settles himself resignedly, with only a feeble flicker of hope that the so-called speech may not be as long as it is thick. The words may be golden, but the hearers' (?) eyes are prone to be leaden, and in about one instance out of a hundred does the perpetrator really deliver an impressive address. His excuse is his apology—he is not to be blamed, as a rule, for some one decreed that it would be dangerous to cut loose from manuscript moorings and take his audience with him on a really delightful sail.

One great trouble on such "great occasions" is that the essayist—for such he is—has been chosen not because of his speaking ability but because his grandfather fought in a certain battle, or his constituents sent him to Congress, or his gifts in some line of endeavor other than speaking have distinguished him.

As well choose a surgeon from his ability to play golf. To be sure, it always interests an audience to see a great man; because of his eminence they are likely to listen to his words with respect, perhaps with interest, even when droned from a manuscript. But how much more effective such a deliverance would be if the papers were cast aside!

Nowhere is the read-address so common as in the pulpit—the pulpit, that in these days least of all can afford to invite a handicap. Doubtless many clergymen prefer finish to fervor—let them choose: they are rarely men who sway the masses to acceptance of their message. What they gain in precision and elegance of language they lose in force.

There are just four motives that can move a man to read his address or sermon:

1. Laziness is the commonest. Enough said. Even Heaven cannot make a lazy man efficient.

2. A memory so defective that he really cannot speak without reading. Alas, he is not speaking when he is reading, so his dilemma is painful—and not to himself alone. But no man has a right to assume that his memory is utterly bad until he has buckled down to memory culture—and failed. A weak memory is oftener an excuse than a reason.

3. A genuine lack of time to do more than write the speech. There are such instances—but they do not occur every week! The disposition of your time allows more flexibility than you realize. Motive 3 too often harnesses up with Motive 1.

4. A conviction that the speech is too important to risk forsaking the manuscript. But, if it is vital that every word should be so precise, the style so polished, and the thoughts so logical, that the preacher must write the sermon entire, is not the message important enough to warrant extra effort in perfecting its delivery? It is an insult to a congregation and disrespectful to Almighty God to put the phrasing of a message above the message itself. To reach the hearts of the hearers the sermon must be delivered—it is only half delivered when the speaker cannot utter it with original fire and force, when he merely repeats words that were conceived hours or weeks before and hence are like champagne that has lost its fizz. The reading preacher's eyes are tied down to his manuscript; he cannot give the audience the benefit of his expression. How long would a play fill a theater if the actors held their cue–books in hand and read their parts? Imagine Patrick Henry reading his famous speech; Peter–the–Hermit, manuscript in hand, exhorting the crusaders; Napoleon, constantly looking at his papers, addressing the army at the Pyramids; or Jesus reading the Sermon on the Mount! These speakers were so full of their subjects, their general preparation had been so richly adequate, that there was no necessity for a manuscript, either to refer to or to serve as "an outward and visible sign" of their preparedness. No event was ever so dignified that it required an *artificial* attempt at speech making. Call an essay by its right name, but never call it a speech. Perhaps the most dignified of events is a supplication to the Creator. If you ever listened to the reading of an original prayer you must have felt its superficiality.

Regardless of what the theories may be about manuscript delivery, the fact remains that it does not work out with efficiency. *Avoid it whenever at all possible.*

This method has certain points in its favor. If you have time and leisure, it is possible to polish and rewrite your ideas until they are expressed in clear, concise terms. Pope sometimes spent a whole day in perfecting one couplet. Gibbon consumed twenty years gathering material for and rewriting the "Decline and Fall of the Roman Empire." Although you cannot devote such painstaking preparation to a speech, you should take time to eliminate useless words, crowd whole paragraphs into a sentence and choose proper illustrations. Good speeches, like plays, are not written; they are rewritten. The National Cash Register Company follows this plan with their most efficient selling organization: they require their salesmen to memorize verbatim a selling talk. They maintain that there is one best way of putting their selling arguments, and they insist that each salesman use this ideal way rather than employ any haphazard phrases that may come into his mind at the moment.

The method of writing and committing has been adopted by many noted speakers; Julius Cæsar, Robert Ingersoll, and, on some occasions, Wendell Phillips, were distinguished examples. The wonderful effects achieved by famous actors were, of course, accomplished through the delivery of memorized lines.

The inexperienced speaker must be warned before attempting this method of delivery that it is difficult and trying. It requires much skill to make it efficient. The memorized lines of the young speaker will usually *sound* like memorized words, and repel.

If you want to hear an example, listen to a department store demonstrator repeat her memorized lingo about the newest furniture polish or breakfast food. It requires training to make a memorized speech sound fresh and spontaneous, and, unless you have a fine native memory, in each instance the finished product necessitates much labor. Should you forget a part of your speech or miss a few words, you are liable to be so confused that, like Mark Twain's guide in Rome, you will be compelled to repeat your lines from the beginning.

On the other hand, you may be so taken up with trying to recall your written words that you will not abandon yourself to the spirit of your address, and so fail to deliver it with that spontaneity which is so vital to forceful delivery.

But do not let these difficulties frighten you. If committing seems best to you, give it a faithful trial. Do not be deterred by its pitfalls, but by resolute practise avoid them.

One of the best ways to rise superior to these difficulties is to do as Dr. Wallace Radcliffe often does: commit without writing the speech, making practically all the preparation mentally, without putting pen to paper—a laborious but effective way of cultivating both mind and memory.

You will find it excellent practise, both for memory and delivery, to commit the specimen speeches found in this volume and declaim them, with all attention to the principles we have put before you. William Ellery Channing, himself a distinguished speaker, years ago had this to say of practise in declamation:

"Is there not an amusement, having an affinity with the drama, which might be usefully introduced among us? I mean, Recitation. A work of genius, recited by a man of fine taste, enthusiasm, and powers of elocution, is a very pure and high gratification. Were this art cultivated and encouraged, great numbers, now insensible to the most beautiful compositions, might be waked up to their excellence and power."

Speaking from Notes

The third, and the most popular method of delivery, is probably also the best one for the beginner. Speaking from notes is not ideal delivery, but we learn to swim in shallow water before going out beyond the ropes.

Make a definite plan for your discourse (for a fuller discussion see Chapter XVIII) and set down the points somewhat in the fashion of a lawyer's brief, or a preacher's outline. Here is a sample of very simple notes:

ATTENTION

I. INTRODUCTION.

Attention indispensable to the performance of any great work. *Anec-dote.*

II. DEFINED AND ILLUSTRATED.

1. From common observation.

2. From the lives of great men {Carlyle, Robert E. Lee.}

III. ITS RELATION TO OTHER MENTAL POWERS.

1. Reason.

2. Imagination.

3. Memory.

4. Will. *Anecdote.*

IV. ATTENTION MAY BE CULTIVATED.

1. Involuntary attention.

2. Voluntary attention. *Examples.*

V. CONCLUSION.

The consequences of inattention and of attention.

Few briefs would be so precise as this one, for with experience a speaker learns to use little tricks to attract his eye—he may underscore a catch–word heavily, draw a red circle around a pivotal idea, enclose the key–word of an anecdote in a wavy–lined box, and so on indefinitely. These points are worth remembering, for nothing so eludes the swift–glancing eye of the speaker as the sameness of typewriting, or even a regular pen–script. So unintentional a thing as a blot on the page may help you to remember a big "point" in your brief—perhaps by association of ideas.

An inexperienced speaker would probably require fuller notes than the specimen given. Yet that way lies danger, for the complete manuscript is but a short remove from the copious outline. Use as few notes as possible.

They may be necessary for the time being, but do not fail to look upon them as a necessary evil; and even when you lay them before you, refer to them only when compelled to do so. Make your notes as full as you please in preparation, but by all means condense them for platform use.

Extemporaneous Speech

Surely this is the ideal method of delivery. It is far and away the most popular with the audience, and the favorite method of the most efficient speakers.

"Extemporaneous speech" has sometimes been made to mean unprepared speech, and indeed it is too often precisely that; but in no such sense do we recommend it strongly to speakers old and young. On the contrary, to speak well without notes requires all the preparation which we discussed so fully in the chapter on "Fluency," while yet relying upon the "inspiration of the hour" for some of your thoughts and much of your language. You had better remember, however, that the most effective inspiration of the hour is the inspiration you yourself bring to it, bottled up in your spirit and ready to infuse itself into the audience.

If you extemporize you can get much closer to your audience. In a sense, they appreciate the task you have before you and send out their sympathy. Extemporize, and you will not have to stop and fumble around amidst your notes—you can keep your eye afire with your message and hold your audience with your very glance. You yourself will feel their response as you read the effects of your warm, spontaneous words, written on their countenances.

Sentences written out in the study are liable to be dead and cold when resurrected before the audience. When you create as you speak you conserve all the native fire of your thought. You can enlarge on one point or omit another, just as the occasion or the mood of the audience may demand. It is not possible for every speaker to use this, the most difficult of all methods of delivery, and least of all can it be used successfully without much practise, but it is the ideal towards which all should strive.

One danger in this method is that you may be led aside from your subject into by–paths. To avoid this peril, firmly stick to your mental outline. Practise speaking from a memorized brief until you gain control. Join a debating society—talk, *talk*, *TALK*, and always extemporize. You may "make a fool of yourself" once or twice, but is that too great a price to pay for success?

Notes, like crutches, are only a sign of weakness. Remember that the power of your speech depends to some extent upon the view your audience holds of you. General Grant's words as president were more powerful than his words as a Missouri farmer. If you would appear in the light of an authority, be one. Make notes on your brain instead of on paper.

Joint Methods of Delivery

A modification of the second method has been adopted by many great speakers, particularly lecturers who are compelled to speak on a wide variety of subjects day after day; such speakers often commit their addresses to memory but keep their manuscripts in flexible book form before them, turning several pages at a time. They feel safer for having a sheet–anchor to windward—but it is an anchor, nevertheless, and hinders rapid, free sailing, though it drag never so lightly.

Other speakers throw out a still lighter anchor by keeping before them a rather full outline of their written and committed speech.

Others again write and commit a few important parts of the address—the introduction, the conclusion, some vital argument, some pat illustration—and depend on the hour for the language of the rest. This method is well adapted to speaking either with or without notes.

Some speakers read from manuscript the most important parts of their speeches and utter the rest extemporaneously.

Thus, what we have called "joint methods of delivery" are open to much personal variation. You must decide for yourself which is best for you, for the occasion, for your subject, for your audience—for these four factors all have their individual claims.

Whatever form you choose, do not be so weakly indifferent as to pre-fer the easy way—choose the *best* way, whatever it cost you in time and effort. And of this be assured: only the practised speaker can hope to gain *both* conciseness of argument and conviction in manner, polish of language and power in delivery, finish of style and fire in utterance.

QUESTIONS AND EXERCISES

1. Which in your judgment is the most suitable of delivery for you? Why?

2. What objections can you offer to, (*a*) memorizing the entire speech; (*b*) reading from manuscript; (*c*) using notes; (*d*) speaking from mem-orized outline or notes; (*ee*) any of the "joint methods"?

3. What is there to commend in delivering a speech in any of the fore-going methods?

4. Can you suggest any combination of methods that you have found efficacious?

5. What methods, according to your observation, do most successful speakers use?

6. Select some topic from the list on page 123, narrow the theme so as to make it specific (see page 122), and deliver a short address, utilizing the four methods mentioned, in four different deliveries of the speech.

7. Select one of the joint methods and apply it to the delivery of the same address.

8. Which method do you prefer, and why?

9. From the list of subjects in the Appendix select a theme and deliv-er a five–minute address without notes, but make careful preparation without putting your thoughts on paper.

NOTE: It is earnestly hoped that instructors will not pass this stage of the work without requiring of their students much practise in the delivery of original speeches, in the manner that seems, after some experiment, to be best suited to the student's gifts. Students who are studying alone should be equally exacting in demand upon themselves. One point is most important: It is easy to learn to read a speech, therefore it is much more urgent that the pupil should have much practise in speaking from notes and speaking without notes. At this stage, pay more attention to manner than to matter—the succeeding chapters take up the composition of the address. Be particularly insistent upon *frequent* and *thorough* review of the principles of delivery discussed in the preceding chapters.

17. Thought And Reserve Power

Providence is always on the side of the last reserve.

—NAPOLEON BONAPARTE.

So mightiest powers by deepest calms are fed,
And sleep, how oft, in things that gentlest be!

—BARRY CORNWALL, *The Sea in Calm.*

What would happen if you should overdraw your bank account? As a rule the check would be protested; but if you were on friendly terms with the bank, your check might be honored, and you would be called upon to make good the overdraft.

Nature has no such favorites, therefore extends no credits. She is as relentless as a gasoline tank—when the "gas" is all used the machine stops. It is as reckless for a speaker to risk going before an audience without having something in reserve as it is for the motorist to essay a long journey in the wilds without enough gasoline in sight.

But in what does a speaker's reserve power consist? In a well-founded reliance on his general and particular grasp of his subject; in the quality of being alert and resourceful in thought—particularly in the ability to think while on his feet; and in that self-possession which makes one the captain of all his own forces, bodily and mental.

The first of these elements, adequate preparation, and the last, self-reliance, were discussed fully in the chapters on "Self-Confidence" and "Fluency," so they will be touched only incidentally here; besides, the next chapter will take up specific methods of preparation for public speaking. Therefore the central theme of this chapter is the second of the elements of reserve power—Thought.

The Mental Storehouse

An empty mind, like an empty larder, may be a serious matter or not—all will depend on the available resources. If there is no food in the cupboard the housewife does not nervously rattle the empty dishes; she telephones the grocer. If you have no ideas, do not rattle your empty *ers* and *ahs*, but *get* some ideas, and don't speak until you do get them.

This, however, is not being what the old New England housekeeper used to call "forehanded." The real solution of the problem of what to do with an empty head is never to let it become empty. In the artesian wells of Dakota the water rushes to the surface and leaps a score of feet above the ground. The secret of this exuberant flow is of course the great supply below, crowding to get out.

What is the use of stopping to prime a mental pump when you can fill your life with the resources for an artesian well? It is not enough to have merely enough; you must have more than enough. Then the pressure of your mass of thought and feeling will maintain your flow of speech and give you the confidence and poise that denote reserve power. To be away from home with only the exact return fare leaves a great deal to circumstances!

Reserve power is magnetic. It does not consist in giving the idea that you are holding something in reserve, but rather in the suggestion that the audience is getting the cream of your observation, reading, experience, feeling, thought. To have reserve power, therefore, you must have enough milk of material on hand to supply sufficient cream.

But how shall we get the milk? There are two ways: the one is first–hand—from the cow; the other is second–hand—from the milkman.

The Seeing Eye

Some sage has said: "For a thousand men who can speak, there is only one who can think; for a thousand men who can think, there is only one who can see." To see and to think is to get your milk from your own cow.

When the one man in a million who can see comes along, we call him Master. Old Mr. Holbrook, of "Cranford," asked his guest what color ash–buds were in March; she confessed she did not know, to which the old gentleman answered: "I knew you didn't. No more did I—an old fool that I am!—till this young man comes and tells me. 'Black as ash–buds in March.' And I've lived all my life in the country. More shame for me not to know. Black; they are jet–black, madam."

"This young man" referred to by Mr. Holbrook was Tennyson.

Henry Ward Beecher said: "I do not believe that I have ever met a man on the street that I did not get from him some element for a sermon. I never see anything in nature which does not work towards that for which I give the strength of my life. The material for my sermons is all the time following me and swarming up around me."

Instead of saying only one man in a million can see, it would strike nearer the truth to say that none of us sees with perfect understanding more than a fraction of what passes before our eyes, yet this faculty of acute and accurate observation is so important that no man ambitious to lead can neglect it. The next time you are in a car, look at those who sit opposite you and see what you can discover of their habits, occupations, ideals, nationalities, environments, education, and so on. You may not see a great deal the first time, but practise will reveal astonishing results. Transmute every incident of your day into a subject for a speech or an illustration. Translate all that you see into terms of speech. When you can describe all that you have seen in definite words, you are seeing clearly. You are becoming the millionth man.

De Maupassant's description of an author should also fit the public–speaker: "His eye is like a suction pump, absorbing everything; like a pickpocket's hand, always at work. Nothing escapes him. He is constantly collecting material, gathering–up glances, gestures, intentions, everything that goes on in his presence—the slightest look, the least act, the merest trifle." De Maupassant was himself a millionth man, a Master.

"Ruskin took a common rock–crystal and saw hidden within its stolid heart lessons which have not yet ceased to move men's lives. Beecher stood for hours before the window of a jewelry store thinking out analogies between jewels and the souls of men. Gough saw in a single drop of water enough truth wherewith to quench the thirst of five thousand souls. Thoreau sat so still in the shadowy woods that birds and insects came and opened up their secret lives to his eye. Emerson observed the soul of a man so long that at length he could say, 'I cannot hear what you say, for seeing what you are.' Preyer for three years studied the life of his babe and so became an authority upon the child mind. Observation! Most men are blind. There are a thousand times as many hidden truths and undiscovered facts about us to–day as have made discoverers famous—facts waiting for some one to 'pluck out the heart of their mystery.' But so long as men go about the search with eyes that see not, so long will these hidden pearls lie in their shells. Not an orator but who could more effectively point and feather his shafts were he to search nature rather than libraries. Too few can see 'sermons in stones' and 'books in the running brooks,' because they are so used to seeing merely sermons in books and only stones in running brooks. Sir Philip Sidney had a saying, 'Look in thy heart and write;' Massillon explained his astute knowledge of the human heart by saying, 'I learned it by studying myself;' Byron says of John Locke that 'all his knowledge of the human understanding was derived from studying his own mind.' Since multiform nature is all about us, originality ought not to be so rare."[8]

The Thinking Mind

Thinking is doing mental arithmetic with facts. Add this fact to that and you reach a certain conclusion. Subtract this truth from another and you have a definite result. Multiply this fact by another and have a precise product. See how many times this occurrence happens in that space of time and you have reached a calculable dividend. In thought–processes you perform every known problem of arithmetic and algebra. That is why mathematics are such excellent mental gymnastics. But by the same token, thinking is work. Thinking takes energy. Thinking requires time, and patience, and broad information, and clearheadedness. Beyond a miserable little surface–scratching, few people really think at all—only one in a thousand, according to the pundit already quoted. So long as the present system of education prevails and children are taught through the ear rather than through the eye, so long as they are expected to remember thoughts of others rather than think for themselves, this proportion will continue—one man in a million will be able to see, and one in a thousand to think.

But, however thought–less a mind has been, there is promise of better things so soon as the mind detects its own lack of thought–power. The first step is to stop regarding thought as "the magic of the mind," to use Byron's expression, and see it as thought truly is—*a weighing of ideas and a placing of them in relationships to each other.* Ponder this definition and see if you have learned to think efficiently.

Habitual thinking is just that—a habit. Habit comes of doing a thing repeatedly. The lower habits are acquired easily, the higher ones require deeper grooves if they are to persist. So we find that the thought–habit comes only with resolute practise; yet no effort will yield richer dividends. Persist in practise, and whereas you have been able to think only an inch–deep into a subject, you will soon find that you can penetrate it a foot.

Perhaps this homely metaphor will suggest how to begin the practise of consecutive thinking, by which we mean *welding a number of separate thought–links into a chain that will hold.* Take one link at a time, see that each naturally belongs with the ones you link to it, and remember that a single missing link means *no chain.*

Thinking is the most fascinating and exhilarating of all mental exercises. Once realize that your opinion on a subject does not represent the choice you have made between what Dr. Cerebrum has written and Professor Cerebellum has said, but is the result of your own earnestly–applied brain–energy, and you will gain a confidence in your ability to speak on that subject that nothing will be able to shake. Your thought will have given you both power and reserve power.

Someone has condensed the relation of thought to knowledge in these pungent, homely lines:

"Don't give me the man who thinks he thinks,
Don't give me the man who thinks he knows,
But give me the man who knows he thinks,
And I have the man who knows he knows!"

Reading As a Stimulus to Thought

No matter how dry the cow, however, nor how poor our ability to milk, there is still the milkman—we can read what others have seen and felt and thought. Often, indeed, such records will kindle within us that pre–essential and vital spark, the *desire* to be a thinker.

The following selection is taken from one of Dr. Newell Dwight Hillis's lectures, as given in "A Man's Value to Society." Dr. Hillis is a most fluent speaker—he never refers to notes. He has reserve power. His mind is a veritable treasure–house of facts and ideas. See how he draws from a knowledge of fifteen different general or special subjects: geology, plant life, Palestine, chemistry, Eskimos, mythology, literature, The Nile, history, law, wit, evolution, religion, biography, and electricity. Surely, it needs no sage to discover that the secret of this man's reserve power is the old secret of our artesian well whose abundance surges from unseen depths.

THE USES OF BOOKS AND READING

Each Kingsley approaches a stone as a jeweler approaches a casket to unlock the hidden gems. Geikie causes the bit of hard coal to unroll the juicy bud, the thick odorous leaves, the pungent boughs, until the bit of carbon enlarges into the beauty of a tropic forest. That little book of Grant Allen's called "How Plants Grow" exhibits trees and shrubs as eating, drinking and marrying. We see certain date groves in Palestine, and other date groves in the desert a hundred miles away, and the pollen of the one carried upon the trade winds to the branches of the other. We see the tree with its strange system of water–works, pumping the sap up through pipes and mains; we see the chemical laboratory in the branches mixing flavor for the orange in one bough, mixing the juices of the pineapple in another; we behold the tree as a mother making each infant acorn ready against the long winter, rolling it in swaths soft and warm as wool blankets, wrapping it around with garments impervious to the rain, and finally slipping the infant acorn into a sleeping bag, like those the Eskimos gave Dr. Kane.

At length we come to feel that the Greeks were not far wrong in thinking each tree had a dryad in it, animating it, protecting it against destruction, dying when the tree withered. Some Faraday shows us that each drop of water is a sheath for electric forces sufficient to charge 800,000 Leyden jars, or drive an engine from Liverpool to London. Some Sir William Thomson tells us how hydrogen gas will chew up a large iron spike as a child's molars will chew off the end of a stick of candy. Thus each new book opens up some new and hitherto unexplored realm of nature. Thus books fulfill for us the legend of the wondrous glass that showed its owner all things distant and all things hidden. Through books our world becomes as "a bud from the bower of God's beauty; the sun as a spark from the light of His wisdom; the sky as a bubble on the sea of His Power." Therefore Mrs. Browning's words, "No child can be called fatherless who has God and his mother; no youth can be called friendless who has God and the companionship of good books."

Books also advantage us in that they exhibit the unity of progress, the solidarity of the race, and the continuity of history. Authors lead us back along the pathway of law, of liberty or religion, and set us down in front of the great man in whose brain the principle had its rise. As the discoverer leads us from the mouth of the Nile back to the head-waters of Nyanza, so books exhibit great ideas and institutions, as they move forward, ever widening and deepening, like some Nile feeding many civilizations. For all the reforms of to–day go back to some re-form of yesterday. Man's art goes back to Athens and Thebes. Man's laws go back to Blackstone and Justinian. Man's reapers and plows go back to the savage scratching the ground with his forked stick, drawn by the wild bullock. The heroes of liberty march forward in a solid col-umn. Lincoln grasps the hand of Washington. Washington received his weapons at the hands of Hampden and Cromwell. The great Puritans lock hands with Luther and Savonarola.

The unbroken procession brings us at length to Him whose Sermon on the Mount was the very charter of liberty. It puts us under a divine spell to perceive that we are all coworkers with the great men, and yet single threads in the warp and woof of civilization. And when books have related us to our own age, and related all the epochs to God, whose providence is the gulf stream of history, these teachers go on to stimulate us to new and greater achievements. Alone, man is an unlighted candle. The mind needs some book to kindle its faculties. Before Byron began to write he used to give half an hour to reading some favorite passage. The thought of some great writer never failed to kindle Byron into a creative glow, even as a match lights the kin-dlings upon the grate. In these burning, luminous moods Byron's mind did its best work. The true book stimulates the mind as no wine can ever quicken the blood. It is reading that brings us to our best, and rouses each faculty to its most vigorous life.

We recognize this as pure cream, and if it seems at first to have its sec-ondary source in the friendly milkman, let us not forget that the theme is "The Uses of Books and Reading." Dr. Hillis both sees and thinks.

It is fashionable just now to decry the value of reading. We read, we are told, to avoid the necessity of thinking for ourselves. Books are for the mentally lazy.

Though this is only a half–truth, the element of truth it contains is large enough to make us pause. Put yourself through a good old Presbyterian soul–searching self–examination, and if reading–from–thought–laziness is one of your sins, confess it. No one can shrive you of it—but yourself. Do penance for it by using your own brains, for it is a transgression that dwarfs the growth of thought and destroys mental freedom. At first the penance will be trying—but at the last you will be glad in it.

Reading should entertain, give information, or stimulate thought. Here, however, we are chiefly concerned with information, and stimulation of thought.

What shall I read for information?

The ample page of knowledge, as Grey tells us, is "rich with the spoils of time," and these are ours for the price of a theatre ticket. You may command Socrates and Marcus Aurelius to sit beside you and discourse of their choicest, hear Lincoln at Gettysburg and Pericles at Athens, storm the Bastile with Hugo, and wander through Paradise with Dante. You may explore darkest Africa with Stanley, penetrate the human heart with Shakespeare, chat with Carlyle about heroes, and delve with the Apostle Paul into the mysteries of faith. The general knowledge and the inspiring ideas that men have collected through ages of toil and experiment are yours for the asking. The Sage of Chelsea was right: "The true university of these days is a collection of books."

To master a worth–while book is to master much else besides; few of us, however, make perfect conquest of a volume without first owning it physically. To read a borrowed book may be a joy, but to assign your own book a place of its own on your own shelves—be they few or many—to love the book and feel of its worn cover, to thumb it over slowly, page by page, to pencil its margins in agreement or in protest, to smile or thrill with its remembered pungencies—no mere book borrower could ever sense all that delight.

The reader who possesses books in this double sense finds also that his books possess him, and the volumes which most firmly grip his life are likely to be those it has cost him some sacrifice to own. These lightly–come–by titles, which Mr. Fatpurse selects, perhaps by proxy, can scarcely play the guide, philosopher and friend in crucial moments as do the books—long coveted, joyously attained—that are welcomed into the lives, and not merely the libraries, of us others who are at once poorer and richer.

So it is scarcely too much to say that of all the many ways in which an owned—a mastered—book is like to a human friend, the truest ways are these: A friend is worth making sacrifices for, both to gain and to keep; and our loves go out most dearly to those into whose inmost lives we have sincerely entered.

When you have not the advantage of the test of time by which to judge books, investigate as thoroughly as possible the authority of the books you read. Much that is printed and passes current is counterfeit. "I read it in a book" is to many a sufficient warranty of truth, but not to the thinker. "What book?" asks the careful mind. "Who wrote it? What does he know about the subject and what right has he to speak on it? Who recognizes him as authority? With what other recognized authorities does he agree or disagree?" Being caught trying to pass counterfeit money, even unintentionally, is an unpleasant situation. Beware lest you circulate spurious coin.

Above all, seek reading that makes you use your own brains. Such reading must be alive with fresh points of view, packed with special knowledge, and deal with subjects of vital interest. Do not confine your reading to what you already know you will agree with. Opposition wakes one up. The other road may be the better, but you will never know it unless you "give it the once over." Do not do all your thinking and investigating in front of given "Q.E.D.'s;" merely assembling reasons to fill in between your theorem and what you want to prove will get you nowhere. Approach each subject with an open mind and—once sure that you have thought it out thoroughly and honestly—have the courage to abide by the decision of your own thought. But don't brag about it afterward.

No book on public speaking will enable you to discourse on the tariff if you know nothing about the tariff. Knowing more about it than the other man will be your only hope for making the other man listen to you.

Take a group of men discussing a governmental policy of which some one says: "It is socialistic." That will commend the policy to Mr. A., who believes in socialism, but condemn it to Mr. B., who does not. It may be that neither had considered the policy beyond noticing that its surface–color was socialistic. The chances are, furthermore, that neither Mr. A. nor Mr. B. has a definite idea of what socialism really is, for as Robert Louis Stevenson says, "Man lives not by bread alone but chiefly by catch words." If you are of this group of men, and have observed this proposed government policy, and investigated it, and thought about it, what you have to say cannot fail to command their respect and approval, for you will have shown them that you possess a grasp of your subject and—to adopt an exceedingly expressive bit of slang—*then* some.

QUESTIONS AND EXERCISES

1. Robert Houdin trained his son to give one swift glance at a shop window in passing and be able to report accurately a surprising number of its contents. Try this several times on different windows and report the result.

2. What effect does reserve power have on an audience?

3. What are the best methods for acquiring reserve power?

4. What is the danger of too much reading?

5. Analyze some speech that you have read or heard and notice how much real information there is in it. Compare it with Dr. Hillis's speech on "Brave Little Belgium," page 394.

6. Write out a three–minute speech on any subject you choose. How much information, and what new ideas, does it contain? Compare your speech with the extract on page 191 from Dr. Hillis's "The Uses of Books and Reading."

7. Have you ever read a book on the practise of thinking? If so, give your impressions of its value.

NOTE: There are a number of excellent books on the subject of thought and the management of thought. The following are recommended as being especially helpful: "Thinking and Learning to Think," Nathan C. Schaeffer; "Talks to Students on the Art of Study," Cramer; "As a Man Thinketh," Allen.

8. Define (*a*) logic; (*b*) mental philosophy (or mental science); (*c*) psy-
chology; (*d*) abstract.

18. Subject And Preparation

Suit your topics to your strength,
And ponder well your subject, and its length;
Nor lift your load, before you're quite aware
What weight your shoulders will, or will not, bear.

—BYRON, *Hints from Horace.*

Look to this day, for it is life—the very life of life. In its brief course lie all the verities and realities of your existence: the bliss of growth, the glory of action, the splendor of beauty. For yesterday is already a dream and tomorrow is only a vision; but today, well lived, makes every yesterday a dream of happiness and every tomorrow a vision of hope. Look well, therefore, to this day. Such is the salutation of the dawn.

—*From the Sanskrit.*

In the chapter preceding we have seen the influence of "Thought and Reserve Power" on general preparedness for public speech. But preparation consists in something more definite than the cultivation of thought–power, whether from original or from borrowed sources—it involves a *specifically* acquisitive attitude of the whole life. If you would become a full soul you must constantly take in and assimilate, for in that way only may you hope to give out that which is worth the hearing; but do not confuse the acquisition of general information with the mastery of specific knowledge. Information consists of a fact or a group of facts; knowledge is *organized* information—knowledge knows a fact in relation to other facts.

Now the important thing here is that you should set all your faculties to take in the things about you with the particular object of correlating them and storing them for use in public speech. You must hear with the speaker's ear, see with the speaker's eye, and choose books and companions sand sights and sounds with the speaker's purpose in view. At the same time, be ready to receive unplanned–for knowledge. One of the fascinating elements in your life as a public speaker will be the conscious growth in power that casual daily experiences bring. If your eyes are alert you will be constantly discovering facts, illustrations, and ideas without having set out in search of them. These all may be turned to account on the platform; even the leaden events of hum–drum daily life may be melted into bullets for future battles.

Conservation of Time in Preparation

But, you say, I have so little time for preparation—my mind must be absorbed by other matters. Daniel Webster never let an opportunity pass to gather material for his speeches. When he was a boy working in a sawmill he read out of a book in one hand and busied himself at some mechanical task with the other. In youth Patrick Henry roamed the fields and woods in solitude for days at a time unconsciously gathering material and impressions for his later service as a speaker. Dr. Russell H. Conwell, the man who, the late Charles A. Dana said, had addressed more hearers than any living man, used to memorize long passages from Milton while tending the boiling syrup–pans in the silent New England woods at night. The modern employer would discharge a Webster of today for inattention to duty, and doubtless he would be justified, and Patrick Henry seemed only an idle chap even in those easy–going days; but the truth remains: those who take in power and have the purpose to use it efficiently will some day win to the place in which that stored–up power will revolve great wheels of influence.

Napoleon said that quarter hours decide the destinies of nations. How many quarter hours do we let drift by aimlessly! Robert Louis Stevenson conserved *all* his time; *every* experience became capital for his work—for capital may be defined as "the results of labor stored up to assist future production." He continually tried to put into suitable language the scenes and actions that were in evidence about him. Emerson says: "Tomorrow will be like today. Life wastes itself whilst we are preparing to live."

Why wait for a more convenient season for this broad, general preparation? The fifteen minutes that we spend on the car could be profitably turned into speech–capital.

Procure a cheap edition of modern speeches, and by cutting out a few pages each day, and reading them during the idle minute here and there, note how soon you can make yourself familiar with the world's best speeches. If you do not wish to mutilate your book, take it with you—most of the epoch–making books are now printed in small volumes. The daily waste of natural gas in the Oklahoma fields is equal to ten thousand tons of coal. Only about three per cent of the power of the coal that enters the furnace ever diffuses itself from your electric bulb as light—the other ninety–seven per cent is wasted. Yet these wastes are no larger, nor more to be lamented than the tremendous waste of time which, if conserved would increase the speaker's powers to their *nth* degree. Scientists are making three ears of corn grow where one grew before; efficiency engineers are eliminating useless motions and products from our factories: catch the spirit of the age and apply efficiency to the use of the most valuable asset you possess—time. What do you do mentally with the time you spend in dressing or in shaving? Take some subject and concentrate your energies on it for a week by utilizing just the spare moments that would otherwise be wasted. You will be amazed at the result. One passage a day from the Book of Books, one golden ingot from some master mind, one fully–possessed thought of your own might thus be added to the treasury of your life. Do not waste your time in ways that profit you nothing. Fill "the unforgiving minute" with "sixty seconds' worth of distance run" and on the platform you will be immeasurably the gainer.

Let no word of this, however, seem to decry the value of recreation. Nothing is more vital to a worker than rest—yet nothing is so vitiating to the shirker. Be sure that your recreation re–creates. A pause in the midst of labors gathers strength for new effort. The mistake is to pause too long, or to fill your pauses with ideas that make life flabby.

Choosing a Subject

Subject and materials tremendously influence each other.

"This arises from the fact that there are two distinct ways in which a subject may be chosen: by arbitrary choice, or by development from thought and reading.

"Arbitrary choice ... of one subject from among a number involves so many important considerations that no speaker ever fails to appreciate the tone of satisfaction in him who triumphantly announces: 'I have a subject!'

"'Do give me a subject!' How often the weary school teacher hears that cry. Then a list of themes is suggested, gone over, considered, and, in most instances, rejected, because the teacher can know but imperfectly what is in the pupil's mind. To suggest a subject in this way is like trying to discover the street on which a lost child lives, by naming over a number of streets until one strikes the little one's ear as sounding familiar.

"Choice by development is a very different process. It does not ask, What shall I say? It turns the mind in upon itself and asks, What do I think? Thus, the subject may be said to choose itself, for in the process of thought or of reading one theme rises into prominence and becomes a living germ, soon to grow into the discourse. He who has not learned to reflect is not really acquainted with his own thoughts; hence, his thoughts are not productive. Habits of reading and reflection will supply the speaker's mind with an abundance of subjects of which he already knows something from the very reading and reflection which gave birth to his theme. This is not a paradox, but sober truth.

"It must be already apparent that the choice of a subject by development savors more of collection than of conscious selection. The subject 'pops into the mind.' ... In the intellect of the trained thinker it concentrates—by a process which we have seen to be induction—the facts and truths of which he has been reading and thinking. This is most often a gradual process. The scattered ideas may be but vaguely connected at first, but more and more they concentrate and take on a single form until at length one strong idea seems to grasp the soul with irresistible force, and to cry aloud, 'Arise, I am your *theme*! Henceforth, until you transmute me by the alchemy of your inward fire into vital speech, you shall know no rest!' Happy, then, is that speaker, for he has found a subject that grips him.

"Of course, experienced speakers use both methods of selection. Even a reading and reflective man is sometimes compelled to hunt for a theme from Dan to Beersheba, and then the task of gathering materials becomes a serious one. But even in such a case there is a sense in which the selection comes by development, because no careful speaker settles upon a theme which does not represent at least some matured thought."

Deciding on the Subject Matter

Even when your theme has been chosen for you by someone else, there remains to you a considerable field for choice of subject matter. The same considerations, in fact, that would govern you in choosing a theme must guide in the selection of the material. Ask yourself—or someone else—such questions as these:

What is the precise nature of the occasion? How large an audience may be expected? From what walks of life do they come? What is their probable attitude toward the theme? Who else will speak? Do I speak first, last, or where, on the program? What are the other speakers going to talk about? What is the nature of the auditorium? Is there a desk? Could the subject be more effectively handled if somewhat modified? Precisely how much time am I to fill?

It is evident that many speech–misfits of subject, speaker, occasion and place are due to failure to ask just such pertinent questions. *What* should be said, by *whom*, and *in what circumstances*, constitute ninety per cent of efficiency in public address. No matter who asks you, refuse to be a square peg in a round hole.

Questions of Proportion

Proportion in a speech is attained by a nice adjustment of time. How fully you may treat your subject it is not always for you to say. Let ten minutes mean neither nine nor eleven—though better nine than eleven, at all events. You wouldn't steal a man's watch; no more should you steal the time of the succeeding speaker, or that of the audience. There is no need to overstep time–limits if you make your preparation adequate and divide your subject so as to give each thought its due proportion of attention—and no more. Blessed is the man that maketh short speeches, for he shall be invited to speak again.

Another matter of prime importance is, what part of your address demands the most emphasis. This once decided, you will know where to place that pivotal section so as to give it the greatest strategic value, and what degree of preparation must be given to that central thought so that the vital part may not be submerged by non–essentials. Many a speaker has awakened to find that he has burnt up eight minutes of a ten–minute speech in merely getting up steam. That is like spending eighty percent of your building–money on the vestibule of the house.

The same sense of proportion must tell you to stop precisely when you are through—and it is to be hoped that you will discover the arrival of that period before your audience does.

Tapping Original Sources

The surest way to give life to speech–material is to gather your facts at first hand. Your words come with the weight of authority when you can say, "I have examined the employment rolls of every mill in this district and find that thirty–two per cent of the children employed are under the legal age." No citation of authorities can equal that. You must adopt the methods of the reporter and find out the facts underlying your argument or appeal. To do so may prove laborious, but it should not be irksome, for the great world of fact teems with interest, and over and above all is the sense of power that will come to you from original investigation. To see and feel the facts you are discussing will react upon you much more powerfully than if you were to secure the facts at second hand.

Live an active life among people who are doing worth–while things, keep eyes and ears and mind and heart open to absorb truth, and then tell of the things you know, as if you know them. The world will listen, for the world loves nothing so much as real life.

How to Use a Library

Unsuspected treasures lie in the smallest library. Even when the owner has read every last page of his books it is only in rare instances that he has full indexes to all of them, either in his mind or on paper, so as to make available the vast number of varied subjects touched upon or treated in volumes whose titles would never suggest such topics.

For this reason it is a good thing to take an odd hour now and then to browse. Take down one volume after another and look over its table of contents and its index. (It is a reproach to any author of a serious book not to have provided a full index, with cross references.) Then glance over the pages, making notes, mental or physical, of material that looks interesting and usable. Most libraries contain volumes that the owner is "going to read some day." A familiarity with even the contents of such books on your own shelves will enable you to refer to them when you want help. Writings read long ago should be treated in the same way—in every chapter some surprise lurks to delight you.

In looking up a subject do not be discouraged if you do not find it indexed or outlined in the table of contents—you are pretty sure to discover some material under a related title.

Suppose you set to work somewhat in this way to gather references on "Thinking:" First you look over your book titles, and there is Schaeffer's "Thinking and Learning to Think." Near it is Kramer's "Talks to Students on the Art of Study"—that seems likely to provide some material, and it does. Naturally you think next of your book on psychology, and there is help there. If you have a volume on the human intellect you will have already turned to it. Suddenly you remember your encyclopedia and your dictionary of quotations—and now material fairly rains upon you; the problem is what *not* to use. In the encyclopedia you turn to every reference that includes or touches or even suggests "thinking;" and in the dictionary of quotations you do the same. The latter volume you find peculiarly helpful because it suggests several volumes to you that are on your own shelves—you never would have thought to look in them for references on this subject. Even fiction will supply help, but especially books of essays and biography. Be aware of your own resources.

To make a general index to your library does away with the necessity for indexing individual volumes that are not already indexed.

To begin with, keep a note–book by you; or small cards and paper cuttings in your pocket and on your desk will serve as well. The same note–book that records the impressions of your own experiences and thoughts will be enriched by the ideas of others.

To be sure, this note–book habit means labor, but remember that more speeches have been spoiled by half–hearted preparation than by lack of talent. Laziness is an own–brother to Over–confidence, and both are your inveterate enemies, though they pretend to be soothing friends.

Conserve your material by indexing every good idea on cards, thus:

[HW: *Socialism* Progress of S., Env. 16 S. a fallacy, 96/210 General article on S., Howells', Dec. 1913 "Socialism and the Franchise," Forbes "Socialism in Ancient Life," Original Ms., Env. 102]

On the card illustrated above, clippings are indexed by giving the number of the envelope in which they are filed. The envelopes may be of any size desired and kept in any convenient receptacle. On the foregoing example, "Progress of S., Envelope 16," will represent a clipping, filed in Envelope 16, which is, of course, numbered arbitrarily.

The fractions refer to books in your library—the numerator being the book–number, the denominator referring to the page. Thus, "S. a fallacy, 96/210," refers to page 210 of volume 96 in your library. By some arbitrary sign—say red ink—you may even index a reference in a public library book.

If you preserve your magazines, important articles may be indexed by month and year. An entire volume on a subject may be indicated like the imaginary book by "Forbes." If you clip the articles, it is better to index them according to the envelope system.

Your own writings and notes may be filed in envelopes with the clippings or in a separate series.

Another good indexing system combines the library index with the "scrap," or clipping, system by making the outside of the envelope serve the same purpose as the card for the indexing of books, magazines, clippings and manuscripts, the latter two classes of material being enclosed in the envelopes that index them, and all filed alphabetically.

When your cards accumulate so as to make ready reference difficult under a single alphabet, you may subdivide each letter by subordinate guide cards marked by the vowels, A, E, I, O, U. Thus, "Antiquities" would be filed under *i* in A, because A begins the word, and the second letter, *n*, comes after the vowel *i* in the alphabet, but before *o*. In the same manner, "Beecher" would be filed under *e* in B; and "Hydrogen" would come under *u* in H.

Outlining the Address

No one can advise you how to prepare the notes for an address. Some speakers get the best results while walking out and ruminating, jotting down notes as they pause in their walk. Others never put pen to paper until the whole speech has been thought out. The great majority, however, will take notes, classify their notes, write a hasty first draft, and then revise the speech. Try each of these methods and choose the one that is best—*for you*. Do not allow any man to force you to work in *his* way; but do not neglect to consider his way, for it may be better than your own.

For those who make notes and with their aid write out the speech, these suggestions may prove helpful:

After having read and thought enough, classify your notes by setting down the big, central thoughts of your material on separate cards or slips of paper. These will stand in the same relation to your subject as chapters do to a book.

Then arrange these main ideas or heads in such an order that they will lead effectively to the result you have in mind, so that the speech may rise in argument, in interest, in power, by piling one fact or appeal upon another until the climax—the highest point of influence on your audience—has been reached.

Next group all your ideas, facts, anecdotes, and illustrations under the foregoing main heads, each where it naturally belongs.

You now have a skeleton or outline of your address that in its polished form might serve either as the brief, or manuscript notes, for the speech or as the guide–outline which you will expand into the written address, if written it is to be.

Imagine each of the main ideas in the brief on page 213 as being separate; then picture your mind as sorting them out and placing them in order; finally, conceive of how you would fill in the facts and examples under each head, giving special prominence to those you wish to emphasize and subduing those of less moment. In the end, you have the outline complete. The simplest form of outline—not very suitable for use on the platform, however—is the following:

WHY PROSPERITY IS COMING

What prosperity means.—The real tests of prosperity.—Its basis in the soil.—American agricultural progress.—New interest in farming.— Enormous value of our agricultural products.—Reciprocal effect on trade.—Foreign countries affected.—Effects of our new internal economy—the regulation of banking and "big business"—on prosperity.—

Effects of our revised attitude toward foreign markets, including our merchant marine.—Summary.

Obviously, this very simple outline is capable of considerable expansion under each head by the addition of facts, arguments, inferences and examples.

Here is an outline arranged with more regard for argument:

FOREIGN IMMIGRATION SHOULD BE RESTRICTED[11]

I. FACT AS CAUSE: Many immigrants are practically paupers.

(Proofs involving statistics or statements of authorities.)

II. FACT AS EFFECT: They sooner or later fill our alms–houses and become public charges. (Proofs involving statistics or statements of authorities.)

III. FACT AS CAUSE: Some of them are criminals. (Examples of recent cases.)

IV. FACT AS EFFECT: They reënforce the criminal classes.

(Effects on our civic life.)

V. FACT AS CAUSE: Many of them know nothing of the duties of free citizenship. (Examples.)

VI. FACT AS EFFECT: Such immigrants recruit the worst element in our politics. (Proofs.)

A more highly ordered grouping of topics and subtopics is shown in the following:

OURS A CHRISTIAN NATION

I. INTRODUCTION: Why the subject is timely. Influences operative against this contention today.

II. CHRISTIANITY PRESIDED OVER THE EARLY HISTORY OF

AMERICA.

1. First practical discovery by a Christian explorer. Columbus worshiped God on the new soil.

2. The Cavaliers.

3. The French Catholic settlers.

4. The Huguenots.

5. The Puritans.

III. THE BIRTH OF OUR NATION WAS UNDER CHRISTIAN AUSPICES.

1. Christian character of Washington.

2. Other Christian patriots.

3. The Church in our Revolutionary struggle. Muhlenberg.

IV. OUR LATER HISTORY HAS ONLY EMPHASIZED OUR NATIONAL ATTITUDE. Examples of dealings with foreign nations show Christian magnanimity. Returning the Chinese Indemnity; fostering the Red Cross; attitude toward Belgium.

V. OUR GOVERNMENTAL FORMS AND MANY OF OUR LAWS ARE OF A CHRISTIAN TEMPER.

1. The use of the Bible in public ways, oaths, etc.

2. The Bible in our schools.

3. Christian chaplains minister to our law–making bodies, to our army, and to our navy.

4. The Christian Sabbath is officially and generally recognized.

5. The Christian family and the Christian system of morality are at the basis of our laws.

VI. THE LIFE OF THE PEOPLE TESTIFIES OF THE POWER OF CHRISTIANITY. Charities, education, etc., have Christian tone.

VII. OTHER NATIONS REGARD US AS A CHRISTIAN PEOPLE.

VIII. CONCLUSION: The attitude which may reasonably be expected of all good citizens toward questions touching the preservation of our standing as a Christian nation.

Writing and Revision

After the outline has been perfected comes the time to write the speech, if write it you must. Then, whatever you do, write it at white heat, with not *too* much thought of anything but the strong, appealing expression of your ideas.

The final stage is the paring down, the re–vision—the seeing again, as the word implies—when all the parts of the speech must be impartially scrutinized for clearness, precision, force, effectiveness, suitability, proportion, logical climax; and in all this you must *imagine yourself to be before your audience*, for a speech is not an essay and what will convince and arouse in the one will not prevail in the other.

The Title

Often last of all will come that which in a sense is first of all—the title, the name by which the speech is known. Sometimes it will be the simple theme of the address, as "The New Americanism," by Henry Watterson; or it may be a bit of symbolism typifying the spirit of the address, as "Acres of Diamonds," by Russell H. Conwell; or it may be a fine phrase taken from the body of the address, as "Pass Prosperity Around," by Albert J. Beveridge. All in all, from whatever motive it be chosen, let the title be fresh, short, suited to the subject, and likely to excite interest.

QUESTIONS AND EXERCISES

1. Define (*a*) introduction; (*b*) climax; (*c*) peroration.

2. If a thirty–minute speech would require three hours for specific preparation, would you expect to be able to do equal justice to a speech one–third as long in one–third the time for preparation? Give reasons.

3. Relate briefly any personal experience you may have had in conserving time for reading and thought.

4. In the manner of a reporter or investigator, go out and get first–hand information on some subject of interest to the public. Arrange the results of your research in the form of an outline, or brief.

5. From a private or a public library gather enough authoritative material on one of the following questions to build an outline for a twenty–minute address. Take one definite side of the question, (*a*) "The Housing of the Poor;" (*b*) "The Commission Form of Government for Cities as a Remedy for Political Graft;" (*c*) "The Test of Woman's Suffrage in the West;" (*d*) "Present Trends of Public Taste in Reading;" (*e*) "Municipal Art;" (*f*) "Is the Theatre Becoming more Elevated in Tone?" (*g*) "The Effects of the Magazine on Literature;" (*h*) "Does Modern Life Destroy Ideals?" (*i*) "Is Competition 'the Life of Trade?'" (*j*) "Baseball is too Absorbing to be a Wholesome National Game;" (*k*) "Summer Baseball and Amateur Standing;" (*l*) "Does College Training Unfit a Woman for Domestic Life?" (*m*) "Does Woman's Competition with Man in Business Dull the Spirit of Chivalry?" (*n*) "Are Elective Studies Suited to High School Courses?" (*o*) "Does the Modern College Prepare Men for Preeminent Leadership?" (*p*) "The Y.M.C.A. in Its Relation to the Labor Problem;" (*q*) "Public Speaking as Training in Citizenship."

6. Construct the outline, examining it carefully for interest, convincing character, proportion, and climax of arrangement.

NOTE:—This exercise should be repeated until the student shows facility in synthetic arrangement.

7. Deliver the address, if possible before an audience.

8. Make a three–hundred word report on the results, as best you are able to estimate them.

9. Tell something of the benefits of using a periodical (or cumulative) index.

10. Give a number of quotations, suitable for a speaker's use, that you have memorized in off moments.

11. In the manner of the outline on page 213, analyze the address on pages 78–79, "The History of Liberty."

12. Give an outline analysis, from notes or memory, of an address or

sermon to which you have listened for this purpose.

13. Criticise the address from a structural point of view.

14. Invent titles for any five of the themes in Exercise 5.

15. Criticise the titles of any five chapters of this book, suggesting better ones.

16. Criticise the title of any lecture or address of which you know.

19. Influencing By Exposition

Speak not at all, in any wise, till you have somewhat to speak; care not for the reward of your speaking, but simply and with undivided mind for the truth of your speaking.

—THOMAS CARLYLE, Essay on *Biography*.

A complete discussion of the rhetorical structure of public speeches requires a fuller treatise than can be undertaken in a work of this nature, yet in this chapter, and in the succeeding ones on "Description," "Narration," "Argument," and "Pleading," the underlying principles are given and explained as fully as need be for a working knowledge, and adequate book references are given for those who would perfect themselves in rhetorical art.

The Nature of Exposition

In the word "expose"—*to lay bare, to uncover, to show the true inwardness of*—we see the foundation–idea of "Exposition." It is the clear and precise setting forth of what the subject really is—it is explanation.

Exposition does not draw a picture, for that would be description. To tell in exact terms what the automobile is, to name its characteristic parts and explain their workings, would be exposition; so would an explanation of the nature of "fear." But to create a mental image of a particular automobile, with its glistening body, graceful lines, and great speed, would be description; and so would a picturing of fear acting on the emotions of a child at night. Exposition and description often intermingle and overlap, but fundamentally they are distinct. Their differences will be touched upon again in the chapter on "Description."

Exposition furthermore does not include an account of how events happened—that is narration. When Peary lectured on his polar discoveries he explained the instruments used for determining latitude and longitude—that was exposition. In picturing his equipment he used description. In telling of his adventures day by day he employed narration. In supporting some of his contentions he used argument. Yet he mingled all these forms throughout the lecture.

Neither does exposition deal with reasons and inferences—that is the field of argument. A series of connected statements intended to convince a prospective buyer that one automobile is better than another, or proofs that the appeal to fear is a wrong method of discipline, would not be exposition. The plain facts as set forth in expository speaking or writing are nearly always the basis of argument, yet the processes are not one. True, the statement of a single significant fact without the addition of one other word may be convincing, but a moment's thought will show that the inference, which completes a chain of reasoning, is made in the mind of the hearer and presupposes other facts held in consideration.

In like manner, it is obvious that the field of persuasion is not open to exposition, for exposition is entirely an intellectual process, with no emotional element.

The Importance of Exposition

The importance of exposition in public speech is precisely the importance of setting forth a matter so plainly that it cannot be misunderstood.

"To master the process of exposition is to become a clear thinker. 'I know, when you do not ask me,' replied a gentleman upon being requested to define a highly complex idea. Now some large concepts defy explicit definition; but no mind should take refuge behind such exceptions, for where definition fails, other forms succeed. Sometimes we feel confident that we have perfect mastery of an idea, but when the time comes to express it, the clearness becomes a haze. Exposition, then, is the test of clear understanding. To speak effectively you must be able to see your subject clearly and comprehensively, and to make your audience see it as you do."

There are pitfalls on both sides of this path. To explain too little will leave your audience in doubt as to what you mean. It is useless to argue a question if it is not perfectly clear just what is meant by the question. Have you never come to a blind lane in conversation by finding that you were talking of one aspect of a matter while your friend was thinking of another? If two do not agree in their definitions of a Musician, it is useless to dispute over a certain man's right to claim the title.

On the other side of the path lies the abyss of tediously explaining too much. That offends because it impresses the hearers that you either do not respect their intelligence or are trying to blow a breeze into a tornado. Carefully estimate the probable knowledge of your audience, both in general and of the particular point you are explaining. In trying to simplify, it is fatal to "sillify." To explain more than is needed for the purposes of your argument or appeal is to waste energy all around. In your efforts to be explicit do not press exposition to the extent of dulness—the confines are not far distant and you may arrive before you know it.

Some Purposes of Exposition

From what has been said it ought to be clear that, primarily, exposition weaves a cord of understanding between you and your audience. It lays, furthermore, a foundation of fact on which to build later statements, arguments, and appeals. In scientific and purely "information" speeches exposition may exist by itself and for itself, as in a lecture on biology, or on psychology; but in the vast majority of cases it is used to accompany and prepare the way for the other forms of discourse.

Clearness, precision, accuracy, unity, truth, and necessity—these must be the *constant* standards by which you test the efficiency of your expositions, and, indeed, that of every explanatory statement. This dictum should be written on your brain in letters most plain. And let this apply not alone to the *purposes* of exposition but in equal measure to your use of the

Methods of Exposition

The various ways along which a speaker may proceed in exposition are likely to touch each other now and then, and even when they do not meet and actually overlap they run so nearly parallel that the roads are sometimes distinct rather in theory than in any more practical respect.

=Definition=, the primary expository method, is a statement of precise limits.Obviously, here the greatest care must be exercised that the terms of definition should not themselves demand too much definition; that the language should be concise and clear; and that the definition should neither exclude nor include too much. The following is a simple example:

To expound is to set forth the nature, the significance, the characteristics, and the bearing of an idea or a group of ideas.

—ARLO BATES, *Talks on Writing English.*

=Contrast and Antithesis= are often used effectively to amplify definition, as in this sentence, which immediately follows the above–cited definition:

Exposition therefore differs from Description in that it deals directly with the meaning or intent of its subject instead of with its appearance.

This antithesis forms an expansion of the definition, and as such it might have been still further extended. In fact, this is a frequent practise in public speech, where the minds of the hearers often ask for reiteration and expanded statement to help them grasp a subject in its several aspects. This is the very heart of exposition—to amplify and clarify all the terms by which a matter is defined.

=Example= is another method of amplifying a definition or of expounding an idea more fully. The following sentences immediately succeed Mr. Bates's definition and contrast just quoted:

A good deal which we are accustomed inexactly to call description is really exposition. Suppose that your small boy wishes to know how an engine works, and should say: "Please describe the steam–engine to me." If you insist on taking his words literally—and are willing to run the risk of his indignation at being wilfully misunderstood—you will to the best of your ability picture to him this familiarly wonderful machine. If you explain it to him, you are not describing but expounding it.

The chief value of example is that it makes clear the unknown by referring the mind to the known. Readiness of mind to make illuminating, apt comparisons for the sake of clearness is one of the speaker's chief resources on the platform—it is the greatest of all teaching gifts. It is a gift, moreover, that responds to cultivation. Read the three extracts from Arlo Bates as their author delivered them, as one passage, and see how they melt into one, each part supplementing the other most helpfully.

=Analogy=, which calls attention to similar relationships in objects not otherwise similar, is one of the most useful methods of exposition. The following striking specimen is from Beecher's Liverpool speech:

A savage is a man of one story, and that one story a cellar. When a man begins to be civilized he raises another story. When you christianize and civilize the man, you put story upon story, for you develop faculty after faculty; and you have to supply every story with your productions.

=Discarding= is a less common form of platform explanation. It consists in clearing away associated ideas so that the attention may be centered on the main thought to be discussed. Really, it is a negative factor in exposition though a most important one, for it is fundamental to the consideration of an intricately related matter that subordinate and side questions should be set aside in order to bring out the main issue. Here is an example of the method:

I cannot allow myself to be led aside from the only issue before this jury. It is not pertinent to consider that this prisoner is the husband of a heartbroken woman and that his babes will go through the world under the shadow of the law's extremest penalty worked upon their father. We must forget the venerable father and the mother whom Heaven in pity took before she learned of her son's disgrace. What have these matters of heart, what have the blenched faces of his friends, what have the prisoner's long and honorable career to say before this bar when you are sworn to weigh only the direct evidence before you? The one and only question for you to decide on the evidence is whether this man did with revengeful intent commit the murder that every impartial witness has solemnly laid at his door.

=Classification= assigns a subject to its class. By an allowable extension of the definition it may be said to assign it also to its order, genus, and species. Classification is useful in public speech in narrowing the issue to a desired phase. It is equally valuable for showing a thing in its relation to other things, or in correlation. Classification is closely akin to Definition and Division.

This question of the liquor traffic, sirs, takes its place beside the grave moral issues of all times. Whatever be its economic significance—and who is there to question it—whatever vital bearing it has upon our political system—and is there one who will deny it?—the question of the licensed saloon must quickly be settled as the world in its advancement has settled the questions of constitutional government for the masses, of the opium traffic, of the serf, and of the slave—not as matters of economic and political expediency but as questions of right and wrong.

=Analysis= separates a subject into its essential parts. This it may do by various principles; for example, analysis may follow the order of time (geologic eras), order of place (geographic facts), logical order (a sermon outline), order of increasing interest, or procession to a climax (a lecture on 20th century poets); and so on. A classic example of analytical exposition is the following:

In philosophy the contemplations of man do either penetrate unto God, or are circumferred to nature, or are reflected or reverted upon himself. Out of which several inquiries there do arise three knowledges: divine philosophy, natural philosophy, and human philosophy or humanity. For all things are marked and stamped with this triple character, of the power of God, the difference of nature, and the use of man.

—LORD BACON, *The Advancement of Learning.*

=Division= differs only from analysis in that analysis follows the inherent divisions of a subject, as illustrated in the foregoing passage, while division arbitrarily separates the subject for convenience of treatment, as in the following none–too–logical example:

For civil history, it is of three kinds; not unfitly to be compared with the three kinds of pictures or images. For of pictures or images, we see some are unfinished, some are perfect, and some are defaced. So of histories we may find three kinds, memorials, perfect histories, and antiquities; for memorials are history unfinished, or the first or rough drafts of history; and antiquities are history defaced, or some remnants of history which have casually escaped the shipwreck of time.

—LORD BACON, *The Advancement of Learning.*

=Generalization= states a broad principle, or a general truth, derived from examination of a considerable number of individual facts. This synthetic exposition is not the same as argumentative generalization, which supports a general contention by citing instances in proof. Observe how Holmes begins with one fact, and by adding another and another reaches a complete whole. This is one of the most effective devices in the public speaker's repertory.

Take a hollow cylinder, the bottom closed while the top remains open, and pour in water to the height of a few inches. Next cover the water with a flat plate or piston, which fits the interior of the cylinder perfectly; then apply heat to the water, and we shall witness the following phenomena. After the lapse of some minutes the water will begin to boil, and the steam accumulating at the upper surface will make room for itself by raising the piston slightly. As the boiling continues, more and more steam will be formed, and raise the piston higher and higher, till all the water is boiled away, and nothing but steam is left in the cylinder. Now this machine, consisting of cylinder, piston, water, and fire, is the steam–engine in its most elementary form. For a steam–engine may be defined as an apparatus for doing work by means of heat applied to water; and since raising such a weight as the piston is a form of doing work, this apparatus, clumsy and inconvenient though it may be, answers the definition precisely.

=Reference to Experience= is one of the most vital principles in exposition—as in every other form of discourse.

"Reference to experience, as here used, means reference to the known. The known is that which the listener has seen, heard, read, felt, believed or done, and which still exists in his consciousness—his stock of knowledge. It embraces all those thoughts, feelings and happenings which are to him real. Reference to Experience, then, means *coming into the listener's life.*

The vast results obtained by science are won by no mystical faculties, by no mental processes, other than those which are practised by every one of us in the humblest and meanest affairs of life. A detective policeman discovers a burglar from the marks made by his shoe, by a mental process identical with that by which Cuvier restored the extinct animals of Montmartre from fragments of their bones. Nor does that process of induction and deduction by which a lady, finding a stain of a particular kind upon her dress, concludes that somebody has upset the inkstand thereon, differ in any way from that by which Adams and Leverrier discovered a new planet. The man of science, in fact, simply uses with scrupulous exactness the methods which we all habitually, and at every moment, use carelessly.

—THOMAS HENRY HUXLEY, *Lay Sermons*.

Do you set down your name in the scroll of youth, that are written down old with all the characters of age? Have you not a moist eye? a dry hand? a yellow cheek? a white beard? a decreasing leg? an increasing belly? is not your voice broken? your wind short? your chin double? your wit single? and every part about you blasted with antiquity? and will you yet call yourself young? Fie, fie, fie, Sir John!

—SHAKESPEARE, *The Merry Wives of Windsor*.

Finally, in preparing expository material ask yourself these questions regarding your subject:

What is it, and what is it not? What is it like, and unlike? What are its causes, and effects? How shall it be divided? With what subjects is it correlated? What experiences does it recall? What examples illustrate it?

QUESTIONS AND EXERCISES

1. What would be the effect of adhering to any one of the forms of discourse in a public address?

2. Have you ever heard such an address?

3. Invent a series of examples illustrative of the distinctions made on pages 232 and 233.

4. Make a list of ten subjects that might be treated largely, if not entirely, by exposition.

5. Name the six standards by which expository writing should be tried.

6. Define any one of the following: (*a*) storage battery; (*b*) "a free hand;" (*c*) sail boat; (*d*) "The Big Stick;" (*e*) nonsense; (*f*) "a good sport;" (*g*) short–story; (*h*) novel; (*i*) newspaper; (*j*) politician; (*k*) jealousy; (*l*) truth; (*m*) matinée girl; (*n*) college honor system; (*o*) modish; (*p*) slum; (*q*) settlement work; (*r*) forensic.

7. Amplify the definition by antithesis.

8. Invent two examples to illustrate the definition (question 6).

9. Invent two analogies for the same subject (question 6).

10. Make a short speech based on one of the following: (*a*) wages and salary; (*b*) master and man; (*c*) war and peace; (*d*) home and the boarding house; (*e*) struggle and victory; (*f*) ignorance and ambition.

11. Make a ten–minute speech on any of the topics named in question 6, using all the methods of exposition already named.

12. Explain what is meant by discarding topics collateral and subordinate to a subject.

13. Rewrite the jury–speech on page 224.

14. Define correlation.

15. Write an example of "classification," on any political, social, economic, or moral issue of the day.

16. Make a brief analytical statement of Henry W. Grady's "The Race Problem," page 36.

17. By what analytical principle did you proceed? (See page 225.)

18. Write a short, carefully generalized speech from a large amount of data on one of the following subjects: (*a*) The servant girl problem; (*b*) cats; (*c*) the baseball craze; (*d*) reform administrations; (*e*) sewing societies; (*f*) coeducation; (*g*) the traveling salesman.

19. Observe this passage from Newton's "Effective Speaking:"

"That man is a cynic. He sees goodness nowhere. He sneers at virtue, sneers at love; to him the maiden plighting her troth is an artful schemer, and he sees even in the mother's kiss nothing but an empty conventionality."

Write, commit and deliver two similar passages based on your choice from this list: (*a*) "the egotist;" (*b*) "the sensualist;" (*c*) "the hypocrite;" (*d*) "the timid man;" (*e*) "the joker;" (*f*) "the flirt;" (*g*) "the ungrateful woman;" (*h*) "the mournful man." In both cases use the principle of "Reference to Experience."

20. Write a passage on any of the foregoing characters in imitation of the style of Shakespeare's characterization of Sir John Falstaff, page 227.

20. Influencing By Description

The groves of Eden vanish'd now so long,
Live in description, and look green in song.

—ALEXANDER POPE, *Windsor Forest.*

The moment our discourse rises above the ground–line of familiar facts, and is inflamed with passion or exalted thought, it clothes itself in images. A man conversing in earnest, if he watch his intellectual processes, will find that always a material image, more or less luminous, arises in his mind, contemporaneous with every thought, which furnishes the vestment of the thought.... This imagery is spontaneous. It is the blending of experience with the present action of the mind. It is proper creation.

—RALPH WALDO EMERSON, *Nature.*

Like other valuable resources in public speaking, description loses its power when carried to an extreme. Over–ornamentation makes the subject ridiculous. A dust–cloth is a very useful thing, but why embroider it? Whether description shall be restrained within its proper and important limits, or be encouraged to run riot, is the personal choice that comes before every speaker, for man's earliest literary tendency is to depict.

The Nature of Description

To describe is to call up a picture in the mind of the hearer. "In talking of description we naturally speak of portraying, delineating, coloring, and all the devices of the picture painter. To describe is to visualize, hence we must look at description as a pictorial process, whether the writer deals with material or with spiritual objects."[20]

If you were asked to describe the rapid–fire gun you might go about it in either of two ways: give a cold technical account of its mechanism, in whole and in detail, or else describe it as a terrible engine of slaughter, dwelling upon its effects rather than upon its structure.

The former of these processes is exposition, the latter is true description. Exposition deals more with the *general*, while description must deal with the *particular*. Exposition elucidates *ideas*, description treats of *things*. Exposition deals with the *abstract*, description with the *concrete*. Exposition is concerned with the *internal*, description with the *external*. Exposition is *enumerative*, description *literary*. Exposition is *intellectual*, description *sensory*. Exposition is *impersonal*, description *personal*.

If description is a visualizing process for the hearer, it is first of all such for the speaker—he cannot describe what he has never seen, either physically or in fancy. It is this personal quality—this question of the personal eye which sees the things later to be described—that makes description so interesting in public speech. Given a speaker of personality, and we are interested in his personal view—his view adds to the natural interest of the scene, and may even be the sole source of that interest to his auditors.

The seeing eye has been praised in an earlier chapter (on "Subject and Preparation") and the imagination will be treated in a subsequent one (on "Riding the Winged Horse"), but here we must consider the *picturing mind*: the mind that forms the double habit of seeing things clearly—for we see more with the mind than we do with the physical eye—and then of re–imaging these things for the purpose of getting them before the minds' eyes of the hearers. No habit is more useful than that of visualizing clearly the object, the scene, the situation, the action, the person, about to be described. Unless that primary process is carried out clearly, the picture will be blurred for the hearer–beholder.

In a work of this nature we are concerned with the rhetorical analysis of description, and with its methods, only so far as may be needed for the practical purposes of the speaker.[21] The following grouping, therefore, will not be regarded as complete, nor will it here be necessary to add more than a word of explanation:

Description for Public Speakers

Objects   { Still
Objects   { In motion
Scenes   { Still

Scenes   { Including action
Situations   { Preceding change
Situations   { During change
Situations   { After change
Actions   { Mental
Actions   {Physical
Persons   { Internal
Persons   { External

Some of the foregoing processes will overlap, in certain instances, and all are more likely to be found in combination than singly.

When description is intended solely to give accurate information—as to delineate the appearance, not the technical construction, of the latest Zeppelin airship—it is called "scientific description," and is akin to exposition. When it is intended to present a free picture for the purpose of making a vivid impression, it is called "artistic description." With both of these the public speaker has to deal, but more frequently with the latter form. Rhetoricians make still further distinctions.

Methods of Description

In public speaking, *description should be mainly by suggestion*, not only because suggestive description is so much more compact and time-saving but because it is so vivid. Suggestive expressions connote more than they literally say—they suggest ideas and pictures to the mind of the hearer which supplement the direct words of the speaker. When Dickens, in his "Christmas Carol," says: "In came Mrs. Fezziwig, one vast substantial smile," our minds complete the picture so deftly begun—a much more effective process than that of a minutely detailed description because it leaves a unified, vivid impression, and that is what we need. Here is a present–day bit of suggestion: "General Trinkle was a gnarly oak of a man—rough, solid, and safe; you always knew where to find him." Dickens presents Miss Peecher as: "A little pin–cushion, a little housewife, a little book, a little work–box, a little set of tables and weights and measures, and a little woman all in one." In his "Knicker-bocker's" "History of New York," Irving portrays Wouter van Twiller as "a robustious beer–barrel, standing on skids."

Whatever forms of description you neglect, be sure to master the art of suggestion.

Description may be by simple hint. Lowell notes a happy instance of this sort of picturing by intimation when he says of Chaucer: "Sometimes he describes amply by the merest hint, as where the Friar, before setting himself down, drives away the cat. We know without need of more words that he has chosen the snuggest corner."

Description may depict a thing by its effects. "When the spectator's eye is dazzled, and he shades it," says Mozley in his "Essays," "we form the idea of a splendid object; when his face turns pale, of a horrible one; from his quick wonder and admiration we form the idea of great beauty; from his silent awe, of great majesty."

Brief description may be by epithet. "Blue–eyed," "white–armed," "laughter–loving," are now conventional compounds, but they were fresh enough when Homer first conjoined them. The centuries have not yet improved upon "Wheels round, brazen, eight–spoked," or "Shields smooth, beautiful, brazen, well–hammered." Observe the effective use of epithet in Will Levington Comfort's "The Fighting Death," when he speaks of soldiers in a Philippine skirmish as being "leeched against a rock."

Description uses figures of speech. Any advanced rhetoric will discuss their forms and give examples for guidance.-This matter is most important, be assured. A brilliant yet carefully restrained figurative style, a style marked by brief, pungent, witty, and humorous comparisons and characterizations, is a wonderful resource for all kinds of platform work.

Description may be direct. This statement is plain enough without exposition. Use your own judgment as to whether in picturing you had better proceed from a general view to the details, or first give the details and thus build up the general picture, but by all means BE BRIEF.

Note the vivid compactness of these delineations from Washington Irving's "Knickerbocker:"

He was a short, square, brawny old gentleman, with a double chin, a mastiff mouth, and a broad copper nose, which was supposed in those days to have acquired its fiery hue from the constant neighborhood of his tobacco pipe.

He was exactly five feet six inches in height, and six feet five inches in circumference. His head was a perfect sphere, and of such stupendous dimensions, that Dame Nature, with all her sex's ingenuity, would have been puzzled to construct a neck capable of supporting it; wherefore she wisely declined the attempt, and settled it firmly on the top of his backbone, just between the shoulders. His body was of an oblong form, particularly capacious at bottom; which was wisely ordered by Providence, seeing that he was a man of sedentary habits, and very averse to the idle labor of walking.

The foregoing is too long for the platform, but it is so good–humored, so full of delightful exaggeration, that it may well serve as a model of humorous character picturing, for here one inevitably sees the inner man in the outer.

Direct description for platform use may be made vivid by the *sparing* use of the "historical present." The following dramatic passage, accompanied by the most lively action, has lingered in the mind for thirty years after hearing Dr. T. De Witt Talmage lecture on "Big Blunders." The crack of the bat sounds clear even today:

Get ready the bats and take your positions. Now, give us the ball. Too low. Don't strike. Too high. Don't strike. There it comes like lightning. Strike! Away it soars! Higher! Higher! Run! Another base! Faster! Faster! Good! All around at one stroke!

Observe the remarkable way in which the lecturer fused speaker, audience, spectators, and players into one excited, ecstatic whole—just as you have found yourself starting forward in your seat at the delivery of the ball with "three on and two down" in the ninth inning. Notice, too, how—perhaps unconsciously—Talmage painted the scene in Homer's characteristic style: not as having already happened, but as happening before your eyes.

If you have attended many travel talks you must have been impressed by the painful extremes to which the lecturers go—with a few notable exceptions, their language is either over–ornate or crude. If you would learn the power of words to make scenery, yes, even houses, palpitate with poetry and human appeal, read Lafcadio Hearn, Robert Louis Stevenson, Pierre Loti, and Edmondo De Amicis.

Blue–distant, a mountain of carven stone appeared before them,—the Temple, lifting to heaven its wilderness of chiseled pinnacles, flinging to the sky the golden spray of its decoration.

—LAFCADIO HEARN, *Chinese Ghosts*.

The stars were clear, colored, and jewel–like, but not frosty. A faint silvery vapour stood for the Milky Way. All around me the black fir–points stood upright and stock–still. By the whiteness of the pack–saddle I could see Modestine walking round and round at the length of her tether; I could hear her steadily munching at the sward; but there was not another sound save the indescribable quiet talk of the runnel over the stones.

—ROBERT LOUIS STEVENSON, *Travels with a Donkey*.

It was full autumn now, late autumn—with the nightfalls gloomy, and all things growing dark early in the old cottage, and all the Breton land looking sombre, too. The very days seemed but twilight; immeasurable clouds, slowly passing, would suddenly bring darkness at broad noon. The wind moaned constantly—it was like the sound of a great cathedral organ at a distance, but playing profane airs, or despairing dirges; at other times it would come close to the door, and lift up a howl like wild beasts.

—PIERRE LOTI, *An Iceland Fisherman*.

I see the great refectory, where a battalion might have drilled; I see the long tables, the five hundred heads bent above the plates, the rapid motion of five hundred forks, of a thousand hands, and sixteen thousand teeth; the swarm of servants running here and there, called to, scolded, hurried, on every side at once; I hear the clatter of dishes, the deafening noise, the voices choked with food crying out: "Bread—bread!" and I feel once more the formidable appetite, the herculean strength of jaw, the exuberant life and spirits of those far–off days.

—EDMONDO DE AMICIS, *College Friends*.

Suggestions for the Use of Description

Decide, on beginning a description, what point of view you wish your hearers to take. One cannot see either a mountain or a man on all sides at once. Establish a view–point, and do not shift without giving notice.

Choose an attitude toward your subject—shall it be idealized? caricatured? ridiculed? exaggerated? defended? or described impartially?

Be sure of your mood, too, for it will color the subject to be described. Melancholy will make a rose–garden look gray.

Adopt an order in which you will proceed—do not shift backward and forward from near to far, remote to close in time, general to particular, large to small, important to unimportant, concrete to abstract, physical to mental; but follow your chosen order. Scattered and shifting observations produce hazy impressions just as a moving camera spoils the time–exposure.

Do not go into needless minutiæ. Some details identify a thing with its class, while other details differentiate it from its class. Choose only the significant, suggestive characteristics and bring those out with terse vividness. Learn a lesson from the few strokes used by the poster artist.

In determining what to describe and what merely to name, seek to read the knowledge of your audience. The difference to them between the unknown and the known is a vital one also to you.

Relentlessly cut out all ideas and words not necessary to produce the effect you desire. Each element in a mental picture either helps or hinders. Be sure they do not hinder, for they cannot be passively present in any discourse.

Interruptions of the description to make side–remarks are as powerful to destroy unity as are scattered descriptive phrases. The only visual impression that can be effective is one that is unified.

In describing, try to call up the emotions you felt when first you saw the scene, and then try to reproduce those emotions in your hearers. Description is primarily emotional in its appeal; nothing can be more deadly dull than a cold, unemotional outline, while nothing leaves a warmer impression than a glowing, spirited description.

Give a swift and vivid general view at the close of the portrayal. First and final impressions remain the longest. The mind may be trained to take in the characteristic points of a subject, so as to view in a single scene, action, experience, or character, a unified impression of the whole. To describe a thing as a whole you must first see it as a whole. Master that art and you have mastered description to the last degree.

SELECTIONS FOR PRACTISE

THE HOMES OF THE PEOPLE

I went to Washington the other day, and I stood on the Capitol Hill; my heart beat quick as I looked at the towering marble of my country's Capitol and the mist gathered in my eyes as I thought of its tremendous significance, and the armies and the treasury, and the judges and the President, and the Congress and the courts, and all that was gathered there. And I felt that the sun in all its course could not look down on a better sight than that majestic home of a republic that had taught the world its best lessons of liberty. And I felt that if honor and wisdom and justice abided therein, the world would at last owe to that great house in which the ark of the covenant of my country is lodged, its final uplifting and its regeneration.

Two days afterward, I went to visit a friend in the country, a modest man, with a quiet country home. It was just a simple, unpretentious house, set about with big trees, encircled in meadow and field rich with the promise of harvest. The fragrance of the pink and hollyhock in the front yard was mingled with the aroma of the orchard and of the gardens, and resonant with the cluck of poultry and the hum of bees.

Inside was quiet, cleanliness, thrift, and comfort. There was the old clock that had welcomed, in steady measure, every newcomer to the family, that had ticked the solemn requiem of the dead, and had kept company with the watcher at the bedside. There were the big, restful beds and the old, open fireplace, and the old family Bible, thumbed with the fingers of hands long since still, and wet with the tears of eyes long since closed, holding the simple annals of the family and the heart and the conscience of the home.

Outside, there stood my friend, the master, a simple, upright man, with no mortgage on his roof, no lien on his growing crops, master of his land and master of himself. There was his old father, an aged, trembling man, but happy in the heart and home of his son. And as they started to their home, the hands of the old man went down on the young man's shoulder, laying there the unspeakable blessing of the honored and grateful father and ennobling it with the knighthood of the fifth commandment.

And as they reached the door the old mother came with the sunset falling fair on her face, and lighting up her deep, patient eyes, while her lips, trembling with the rich music of her heart, bade her husband and son welcome to their home. Beyond was the housewife, busy with her household cares, clean of heart and conscience, the buckler and helpmeet of her husband. Down the lane came the children, trooping home after the cows, seeking as truant birds do the quiet of their home nest.

And I saw the night come down on that house, falling gently as the wings of the unseen dove. And the old man—while a startled bird called from the forest, and the trees were shrill with the cricket's cry, and the stars were swarming in the sky—got the family around him, and, taking the old Bible from the table, called them to their knees, the little baby hiding in the folds of its mother's dress, while he closed the record of that simple day by calling down God's benediction on that family and that home. And while I gazed, the vision of that marble Capitol faded. Forgotten were its treasures and its majesty and I said, "Oh, surely here in the homes of the people are lodged at last the strength and the responsibility of this government, the hope and the promise of this republic."

—HENRY W. GRADY.

SUGGESTIVE SCENES

One thing in life calls for another; there is a fitness in events and places. The sight of a pleasant arbor puts it in our mind to sit there. One place suggests work, another idleness, a third early rising and long rambles in the dew. The effect of night, of any flowing water, of lighted cities, of the peep of day, of ships, of the open ocean, calls up in the mind an army of anonymous desires and pleasures. Something, we feel, should happen; we know not what, yet we proceed in quest of it. And many of the happiest hours in life fleet by us in this vain attendance on the genius of the place and moment. It is thus that tracts of young fir, and low rocks that reach into deep soundings, particularly delight and torture me. Something must have happened in such places, and perhaps ages back, to members of my race; and when I was a child I tried to invent appropriate games for them, as I still try, just as vainly, to fit them with the proper story. Some places speak distinctly. Certain dank gardens cry aloud for a murder; certain old houses demand to be haunted; certain coasts are set aside for shipwreck. Other spots again seem to abide their destiny, suggestive and impenetrable, "miching mallecho." The inn at Burford Bridge, with its arbours and green garden and silent, eddying river—though it is known already as the place where Keats wrote some of his *Endymion* and Nelson parted from his Emma—still seems to wait the coming of the appropriate legend. Within these ivied walls, behind these old green shutters, some further business smoulders, waiting for its hour. The old Hawes Inn at the Queen's ferry makes a similar call upon my fancy. There it stands, apart from the town, beside the pier, in a climate of its own, half inland, half marine—in front, the ferry bubbling with the tide and the guard–ship swinging to her anchor; behind, the old garden with the trees. Americans seek it already for the sake of Lovel and Oldbuck, who dined there at the beginning of the *Antiquary*. But you need not tell me—that is not all; there is some story, unrecorded or not yet complete, which must express the meaning of that inn more fully.... I have lived both at the Hawes and Burford in a perpetual flutter, on the heel, as it seemed, of some adventure that should justify the place; but though the feeling had me to bed at night and called me again at morning in one unbroken round of pleasure and suspense, nothing befell me in either worth remark. The man or the hour had not yet come; but some day, I think, a boat shall put off from the Queen's ferry, fraught with a dear cargo, and some frosty night a horseman, on a tragic errand, rattle with his whip upon the green shutters at the inn at Burford.

—R.L. STEVENSON, *A Gossip on Romance.*

FROM "MIDNIGHT IN LONDON"

Clang! Clang! Clang! the fire–bells! Bing! Bing! Bing! the alarm! In an instant quiet turns to uproar—an outburst of noise, excitement, clamor—bedlam broke loose; Bing! Bing! Bing! Rattle, clash and clatter. Open fly the doors; brave men mount their boxes. Bing! Bing! Bing! They're off! The horses tear down the street like mad. Bing! Bing! Bing! goes the gong!

"Get out of the track! The engines are coming! For God's sake, snatch that child from the road!"

On, on, wildly, resolutely, madly fly the steeds. Bing! Bing! the gong. Away dash the horses on the wings of fevered fury. On whirls the machine, down streets, around corners, up this avenue and across that one, out into the very bowels of darkness, whiffing, wheezing, shooting a million sparks from the stack, paving the path of startled night with a galaxy of stars. Over the house–tops to the north, a volcanic burst of flame shoots out, belching with blinding effect. The sky is ablaze. A tenement house is burning. Five hundred souls are in peril. Merciful Heaven! Spare the victims! Are the engines coming? Yes, here they are, dashing down the street. Look! the horses ride upon the wind; eyes bulging like balls of fire; nostrils wide open. A palpitating billow of fire, rolling, plunging, bounding rising, falling, swelling, heaving, and with mad passion bursting its red–hot sides asunder, reaching out its arms, encircling, squeezing, grabbing up, swallowing everything before it with the hot, greedy mouth of an appalling monster.

How the horses dash around the corner! Animal instinct say you? Aye, more. Brute reason.

"Up the ladders, men!"

The towering building is buried in bloated banks of savage, biting elements. Forked tongues dart out and in, dodge here and there, up and down, and wind their cutting edges around every object. A crash, a dull, explosive sound, and a puff of smoke leaps out. At the highest point upon the roof stands a dark figure in a desperate strait, the hands making frantic gestures, the arms swinging wildly—and then the body shoots off into frightful space, plunging upon the pavement with a revolting thud. The man's arm strikes a bystander as he darts down. The crowd shudders, sways, and utters a low murmur of pity and horror. The faint–hearted lookers–on hide their faces. One woman swoons away.

"Poor fellow! Dead!" exclaims a laborer, as he looks upon the man's body.

"Aye, Joe, and I knew him well, too! He lived next door to me, five flights back. He leaves a widowed mother and two wee bits of orphans. I helped him bury his wife a fortnight ago. Ah, Joe! but it's hard lines for the orphans."

A ghastly hour moves on, dragging its regiment of panic in its trail and leaving crimson blotches of cruelty along the path of night.

"Are they all out, firemen?"

"Aye, aye, sir!"

"No, they're not! There's a woman in the top window holding a child in her arms—over yonder in the right–hand corner! The ladders, there! A hundred pounds to the man who makes the rescue!"

A dozen start. One man more supple than the others, and reckless in his bravery, clambers to the top rung of the ladder.

"Too short!" he cries. "Hoist another!"

Up it goes. He mounts to the window, fastens the rope, lashes mother and babe, swings them off into ugly emptiness, and lets them down to be rescued by his comrades.

"Bravo, fireman!" shouts the crowd.

A crash breaks through the uproar of crackling timbers.

"Look alive, up there! Great God! The roof has fallen!"

The walls sway, rock, and tumble in with a deafening roar. The spectators cease to breathe. The cold truth reveals itself. The fireman has been carried into the seething furnace. An old woman, bent with the weight of age, rushes through the fire line, shrieking, raving, and wringing her hands and opening her heart of grief.

"Poor John! He was all I had! And a brave lad he was, too! But he's gone now. He lost his own life in savin' two more, and now—now he's there, away in there!" she repeats, pointing to the cruel oven.

The engines do their work. The flames die out. An eerie gloom hangs over the ruins like a formidable, blackened pall.

And the noon of night is passed.

—ARDENNES JONES–FOSTER.

QUESTIONS AND ANSWERS

1. Write two paragraphs on one of these: the race horse, the motor boat, golfing, tennis; let the first be pure exposition and the second pure description.

2. Select your own theme and do the same in two short extemporaneous speeches.

3. Deliver a short original address in the over–ornamented style.

4. (*a*) Point out its defects; (*b*) recast it in a more effective style; (*c*) show how the one surpasses the other.

5. Make a list of ten subjects which lend themselves to description in the style you prefer.

6. Deliver a two–minute speech on any one of them, using chiefly, but not solely, description.

7. For one minute, look at any object, scene, action, picture, or person you choose, take two minutes to arrange your thoughts, and then deliver a short description—all without making written notes.

8. In what sense is description more *personal* than exposition?

9. Explain the difference between a scientific and an artistic description.

10. In the style of Dickens and Irving (pages 234, 235), write five separate sentences describing five characters by means of suggestion—one sentence to each.

11. Describe a character by means of a hint, after the manner of Chaucer (p. 235).

12. Read aloud the following with special attention to gesture:

His very throat was moral. You saw a good deal of it. You looked over a very low fence of white cravat (whereof no man had ever beheld the tie, for he fastened it behind), and there it lay, a valley between two jutting heights of collar, serene and whiskerless before you. It seemed to say, on the part of Mr. Pecksniff, "There is no deception, ladies and gentlemen, all is peace, a holy calm pervades me." So did his hair, just grizzled with an iron gray, which was all brushed off his forehead, and stood bolt upright, or slightly drooped in kindred action with his heavy eyelids. So did his person, which was sleek though free from corpulency. So did his manner, which was soft and oily. In a word, even his plain black suit, and state of widower, and dangling double eye–glass, all tended to the same purpose, and cried aloud, "Behold the moral Pecksniff!"

—CHARLES DICKENS, *Martin Chuzzlewit.*

13. Which of the following do you prefer, and why?

She was a blooming lass of fresh eighteen, plump as a partridge, ripe and melting and rosy–cheeked as one of her father's peaches.

—IRVING.

She was a splendidly feminine girl, as wholesome as a November pip-pin, and no more mysterious than a window–pane.

—O. HENRY.

Small, shining, neat, methodical, and buxom was Miss Peecher; cherry–cheeked and tuneful of voice.

—DICKENS.

14. Invent five epithets, and apply them as you choose (p. 235).

15. (*a*) Make a list of five figures of speech; (*b*) define them; (*c*) give an example—preferably original—under each.

16. Pick out the figures of speech in the address by Grady, on page 240.

17. Invent an original figure to take the place of any one in Grady's speech.

18. What sort of figures do you find in the selection from Stevenson, on page 242?

19. What methods of description does he seem to prefer?

20. Write and deliver, without notes and with descriptive gestures, a description in imitation of any of the authors quoted in this chapter.

21. Reëxamine one of your past speeches and improve the descriptive work. Report on what faults you found to exist.

22. Deliver an extemporaneous speech describing any dramatic scene in the style of "Midnight in London."

23. Describe an event in your favorite sport in the style of Dr. Talmage. Be careful to make the delivery effective.

24. Criticise, favorably or unfavorably, the descriptions of any travel talk you may have heard recently.

25. Deliver a brief original travel talk, as though you were showing pictures.

26. Recast the talk and deliver it "without pictures."

21. Influencing By Narration

The art of narration is the art of writing in hooks and eyes. The principle consists in making the appropriate thought follow the appropriate thought, the proper fact the proper fact; in first preparing the mind for what is to come, and then letting it come.

—WALTER BAGEHOT, *Literary Studies.*

Our very speech is curiously historical. Most men, you may observe, speak only to narrate; not in imparting what they have thought, which indeed were often a very small matter, but in exhibiting what they have undergone or seen, which is a quite unlimited one, do talkers dilate. Cut us off from Narrative, how would the stream of conversation, even among the wisest, languish into detached handfuls, and among the foolish utterly evaporate! Thus, as we do nothing but enact History, we say little but recite it.

—THOMAS CARLYLE, *On History.*

Only a small segment of the great field of narration offers its resources to the public speaker, and that includes the anecdote, biographical facts, and the narration of events in general.

Narration—more easily defined than mastered—is the recital of an incident, or a group of facts and occurrences, in such a manner as to produce a desired effect.

The laws of narration are few, but its successful practise involves more of art than would at first appear—so much, indeed, that we cannot even touch upon its technique here, but must content ourselves with an examination of a few examples of narration as used in public speech.

In a preliminary way, notice how radically the public speaker's use of narrative differs from that of the story–writer in the more limited scope, absence of extended dialogue and character drawing, and freedom from elaboration of detail, which characterize platform narrative. On the other hand, there are several similarities of method: the frequent combination of narration with exposition, description, argumentation, and pleading; the care exercised in the arrangement of material so as to produce a strong effect at the close (climax); the very general practise of concealing the "point" (dénouement) of a story until the effective moment; and the careful suppression of needless, and therefore hurtful, details.

So we see that, whether for magazine or platform, the art of narration involves far more than the recital of annals; the succession of events recorded requires a *plan* in order to bring them out with real effect.

It will be noticed, too, that the literary style in platform narration is likely to be either less polished and more vigorously dramatic than in that intended for publication, or else more fervid and elevated in tone. In this latter respect, however, the best platform speaking of today differs from the models of the preceding generation, wherein a highly dignified, and sometimes pompous, style was thought the only fitting dress for a public deliverance. Great, noble and stirring as these older masters were in their lofty and impassioned eloquence, we are sometimes oppressed when we read their sounding periods for any great length of time—even allowing for all that we lose by missing the speaker's presence, voice, and fire. So let us model our platform narration, as our other forms of speech, upon the effective addresses of the moderns, without lessening our admiration for the older school.

The Anecdote

An anecdote is a short narrative of a single event, told as being striking enough to bring out a point. The keener the point, the more condensed the form, and the more suddenly the application strikes the hearer, the better the story.

To regard an anecdote as an illustration—an interpretive picture—will help to hold us to its true purpose, for a purposeless story is of all offenses on the platform the most asinine. A perfectly capital joke will fall flat when it is dragged in by the nape without evident bearing on the subject under discussion. On the other hand, an apposite anecdote has saved many a speech from failure.

"There is no finer opportunity for the display of tact than in the introduction of witty or humorous stories into a discourse. Wit is keen and like a rapier, piercing deeply, sometimes even to the heart. Humor is good-natured, and does not wound. Wit is founded upon the sudden discovery of an unsuspected relation existing between two ideas. Humor deals with things out of relation—with the incongruous. It was wit in Douglass Jerrold to retort upon the scowl of a stranger whose shoulder he had familiarly slapped, mistaking him for a friend: 'I beg your pardon, I thought I knew you—but I'm glad I don't.' It was humor in the Southern orator, John Wise, to liken the pleasure of spending an evening with a Puritan girl to that of sitting on a block of ice in winter, cracking hailstones between his teeth."

The foregoing quotation has been introduced chiefly to illustrate the first and simplest form of anecdote—the single sentence embodying a pungent saying.

Another simple form is that which conveys its meaning without need of "application," as the old preachers used to say. George Ade has quoted this one as the best joke he ever heard:

Two solemn-looking gentlemen were riding together in a railway carriage. One gentleman said to the other: "Is your wife entertaining this summer?" Whereupon the other gentleman replied: "Not very."

Other anecdotes need harnessing to the particular truth the speaker wishes to carry along in his talk. Sometimes the application is made before the story is told and the audience is prepared to make the comparison, point by point, as the illustration is told. Henry W. Grady used this method in one of the anecdotes he told while delivering his great extemporaneous address, "The New South."

Age does not endow all things with strength and virtue, nor are all new things to be despised. The shoemaker who put over his door, "John Smith's shop, founded 1760," was more than matched by his young rival across the street who hung out this sign: "Bill Jones. Established 1886. No old stock kept in this shop."

In two anecdotes, told also in "The New South," Mr. Grady illustrated another way of enforcing the application: in both instances he split the idea he wished to drive home, bringing in part before and part after the recital of the story. The fact that the speaker misquoted the words of Genesis in which the Ark is described did not seem to detract from the burlesque humor of the story.

I bespeak the utmost stretch of your courtesy tonight. I am not troubled about those from whom I come. You remember the man whose wife sent him to a neighbor with a pitcher of milk, who, tripping on the top step, fell, with such casual interruptions as the landings afforded, into the basement, and, while picking himself up, had the pleasure of hearing his wife call out:

"John, did you break the pitcher?

"No, I didn't," said John, "but I be dinged if I don't."

So, while those who call to me from behind may inspire me with energy, if not with courage, I ask an indulgent hearing from you. I beg that you will bring your full faith in American fairness and frankness to judgment upon what I shall say. There was an old preacher once who told some boys of the Bible lesson he was going to read in the morning. The boys, finding the place, glued together the connecting pages. The next morning he read on the bottom of one page: "When Noah was one hundred and twenty years old he took unto himself a wife, who was"—then turning the page - "one hundred and forty cubits long, forty cubits wide, built of gopher wood, and covered with pitch inside and out." He was naturally puzzled at this. He read it again, verified it, and then said, "My friends, this is the first time I ever met this in the Bible, but I accept it as an evidence of the assertion that we are fearfully and wonderfully made." If I could get you to hold such faith to-night, I could proceed cheerfully to the task I otherwise approach with a sense of consecration.

Now and then a speaker will plunge without introduction into an anecdote, leaving the application to follow. The following illustrates this method:

A large, slew-footed darky was leaning against the corner of the railroad station in a Texas town when the noon whistle in the canning factory blew and the hands hurried out, bearing their grub buckets. The darky listened, with his head on one side until the rocketing echo had quite died away. Then he heaved a deep sigh and remarked to himself:

"Dar she go. Dinner time for some folks—but jes' 12 o'clock fur me!"

That is the situation in thousands of American factories, large and small, today. And why? etc., etc.

Doubtless the most frequent platform use of the anecdote is in the pulpit. The sermon "illustration," however, is not always strictly narrative in form, but tends to extended comparison, as the following from Dr. Alexander Maclaren:

Men will stand as Indian fakirs do, with their arms above their heads until they stiffen there. They will perch themselves upon pillars like Simeon Stylites, for years, till the birds build their nests in their hair. They will measure all the distance from Cape Comorin to Juggernaut's temple with their bodies along the dusty road. They will wear hair shirts and scourge themselves. They will fast and deny themselves. They will build cathedrals and endow churches. They will do as many of you do, labor by fits and starts all thru your lives at the endless task of making yourselves ready for heaven, and winning it by obedience and by righteousness. They will do all these things and do them gladly, rather than listen to the humbling message that says, "You do not need to do anything—wash." Is it your washing, or the water, that will clean you? Wash and be clean! Naaman's cleaning was only a test of his obedience, and a token that it was God who cleansed him. There was no power in Jordan's waters to take away the taint of leprosy. Our cleansing is in that blood of Jesus Christ that has the power to take away all sin, and to make the foulest amongst us pure and clean.

One final word must be said about the introduction to the anecdote. A clumsy, inappropriate introduction is fatal, whereas a single apt or witty sentence will kindle interest and prepare a favorable hearing. The following extreme illustration, by the English humorist, Captain Harry Graham, well satirizes the stumbling manner:

The best story that I ever heard was one that I was told once in the fall of 1905 (or it may have been 1906), when I was visiting Boston—at least, I think it was Boston; it may have been Washington (my memory is so bad).

I happened to run across a most amusing man whose name I forget—Williams or Wilson or Wilkins; some name like that—and he told me this story while we were waiting for a trolley car.

I can still remember how heartily I laughed at the time; and again, that evening, after I had gone to bed, how I laughed myself to sleep recalling the humor of this incredibly humorous story. It was really quite extraordinarily funny. In fact, I can truthfully affirm that it is quite the most amusing story I have ever had the privilege of hearing. Unfortunately, I've forgotten it.

Biographical Facts

Public speaking has much to do with personalities; naturally, therefore, the narration of a series of biographical details, including anecdotes among the recital of interesting facts, plays a large part in the eulogy, the memorial address, the political speech, the sermon, the lecture, and other platform deliverances. Whole addresses may be made up of such biographical details, such as a sermon on "Moses," or a lecture on "Lee."

The following example is in itself an expanded anecdote, forming a link in a chain:

MARIUS IN PRISON

The peculiar sublimity of the Roman mind does not express itself, nor is it at all to be sought, in their poetry. Poetry, according to the Roman ideal of it, was not an adequate organ for the grander movements of the national mind. Roman sublimity must be looked for in Roman acts, and in Roman sayings. Where, again, will you find a more adequate expression of the Roman majesty, than in the saying of Trajan—*Imperatorem oportere stantem mori*—that Cæsar ought to die standing; a speech of imperatorial grandeur! Implying that he, who was "the foremost man of all this world,"—and, in regard to all other nations, the representative of his own,—should express its characteristic virtue in his farewell act—should die *in procinctu*—and should meet the last enemy as the first, with a Roman countenance and in a soldier's attitude. If this had an imperatorial—what follows had a consular majesty, and is almost the grandest story upon record.

Marius, the man who rose to be seven times consul, was in a dungeon, and a slave was sent in with commission to put him to death. These were the persons,—the two extremities of exalted and forlorn humanity, its vanward and its rearward man, a Roman consul and an abject slave. But their natural relations to each other were, by the caprice of fortune, monstrously inverted: the consul was in chains; the slave was for a moment the arbiter of his fate. By what spells, what magic, did Marius reinstate himself in his natural prerogatives? By what marvels drawn from heaven or from earth, did he, in the twinkling of an eye, again invest himself with the purple, and place between himself and his assassin a host of shadowy lictors? By the mere blank supremacy of great minds over weak ones. He *fascinated* the slave, as a rattlesnake does a bird. Standing "like Teneriffe," he smote him with his eye, and said, *"Tune, homo, audes occidere C. Marium?"* - "Dost thou, fellow, presume to kill Caius Marius?" Whereat, the reptile, quaking under the voice, nor daring to affront the consular eye, sank gently to the ground—turned round upon his hands and feet—and, crawling out of the prison like any other vermin, left Marius standing in solitude as steadfast and immovable as the capitol.

—THOMAS DE QUINCY.

Here is a similar example, prefaced by a general historical statement and concluding with autobiographical details:

A REMINISCENCE OF LEXINGTON

One raw morning in spring—it will be eighty years the 19th day of this month—Hancock and Adams, the Moses and Aaron of that Great Deliverance, were both at Lexington; they also had "obstructed an of-ficer" with brave words. British soldiers, a thousand strong, came to seize them and carry them over sea for trial, and so nip the bud of Freedom auspiciously opening in that early spring. The town militia came together before daylight, "for training." A great, tall man, with a large head and a high, wide brow, their captain,—one who had "seen service,"—marshalled them into line, numbering but seventy, and bade "every man load his piece with powder and ball. I will order the first man shot that runs away," said he, when some faltered. "Don't fire unless fired upon, but if they want to have a war, let it begin here."

Gentlemen, you know what followed; those farmers and mechanics "fired the shot heard round the world." A little monument covers the bones of such as before had pledged their fortune and their sacred honor to the Freedom of America, and that day gave it also their lives. I was born in that little town, and bred up amid the memories of that day. When a boy, my mother lifted me up, one Sunday, in her religious, patriotic arms, and held me while I read the first monumental line I ever saw - "Sacred to Liberty and the Rights of Mankind."

Since then I have studied the memorial marbles of Greece and Rome, in many an ancient town; nay, on Egyptian obelisks have read what was written before the Eternal raised up Moses to lead Israel out of Egypt; but no chiseled stone has ever stirred me to such emotion as these rustic names of men who fell "In the Sacred Cause of God and their Country."

Gentlemen, the Spirit of Liberty, the Love of Justice, were early fanned into a flame in my boyish heart. That monument covers the bones of my own kinsfolk; it was their blood which reddened the long, green grass at Lexington. It was my own name which stands chiseled on that stone; the tall captain who marshalled his fellow farmers and mechanics into stern array, and spoke such brave and dangerous words as opened the war of American Independence,—the last to leave the field,—was my father's father. I learned to read out of his Bible, and with a musket he that day captured from the foe, I learned another religious lesson, that "Rebellion to Tyrants is Obedience to God." I keep them both "Sacred to Liberty and the Rights of Mankind," to use them both "In the Sacred Cause of God and my Country."

—THEODORE PARKER.

Narration of Events in General

In this wider, emancipated narration we find much mingling of other forms of discourse, greatly to the advantage of the speech, for this truth cannot be too strongly emphasized: The efficient speaker cuts loose from form for the sake of a big, free effect. The present analyses are for no other purpose than to *acquaint* you with form—do not allow any such models to hang as a weight about your neck.

The following pure narration of events, from George William Curtis's "Paul Revere's Ride," varies the biographical recital in other parts of his famous oration:

That evening, at ten o'clock, eight hundred British troops, under Lieutenant–Colonel Smith, took boat at the foot of the Common and crossed to the Cambridge shore. Gage thought his secret had been kept, but Lord Percy, who had heard the people say on the Common that the troops would miss their aim, undeceived him. Gage instantly ordered that no one should leave the town. But as the troops crossed the river, Ebenezer Dorr, with a message to Hancock and Adams, was riding over the Neck to Roxbury, and Paul Revere was rowing over the river to Charlestown, having agreed with his friend, Robert Newman, to show lanterns from the belfry of the Old North Church - "One if by land, and two if by sea"—as a signal of the march of the British.

The following, from the same oration, beautifully mingles description with narration:

It was a brilliant night. The winter had been unusually mild, and the spring very forward. The hills were already green. The early grain waved in the fields, and the air was sweet with the blossoming orchards. Already the robins whistled, the bluebirds sang, and the benediction of peace rested upon the landscape. Under the cloudless moon the soldiers silently marched, and Paul Revere swiftly rode, galloping through Medford and West Cambridge, rousing every house as he went spurring for Lexington and Hancock and Adams, and evading the British patrols who had been sent out to stop the news.

In the succeeding extract from another of Mr. Curtis's addresses, we have a free use of allegory as illustration:

THE LEADERSHIP OF EDUCATED MEN

There is a modern English picture which the genius of Hawthorne might have inspired. The painter calls it, "How they met themselves." A man and a woman, haggard and weary, wandering lost in a somber wood, suddenly meet the shadowy figures of a youth and a maid. Some mysterious fascination fixes the gaze and stills the hearts of the wanderers, and their amazement deepens into awe as they gradually recognize themselves as once they were; the soft bloom of youth upon their rounded cheeks, the dewy light of hope in their trusting eyes, exulting confidence in their springing step, themselves blithe and radiant with the glory of the dawn. Today, and here, we meet ourselves. Not to these familiar scenes alone—yonder college–green with its reverend traditions; the halcyon cove of the Seekonk, upon which the memory of Roger Williams broods like a bird of calm; the historic bay, beating forever with the muffled oars of Barton and of

Abraham Whipple; here, the humming city of the living; there, the peaceful city of the dead;—not to these only or chiefly do we return, but to ourselves as we once were. It is not the smiling freshmen of the year, it is your own beardless and unwrinkled faces, that are looking from the windows of University Hall and of Hope College. Under the trees upon the hill it is yourselves whom you see walking, full of hopes and dreams, glowing with conscious power, and "nourishing a youth sublime;" and in this familiar temple, which surely has never echoed with eloquence so fervid and inspiring as that of your commencement orations, it is not yonder youths in the galleries who, as they fondly believe, are whispering to yonder maids; it is your younger selves who, in the days that are no more, are murmuring to the fairest mothers and grandmothers of those maids.

Happy the worn and weary man and woman in the picture could they have felt their older eyes still glistening with that earlier light, and their hearts yet beating with undiminished sympathy and aspiration. Happy we, brethren, whatever may have been achieved, whatever left undone, if, returning to the home of our earlier years, we bring with us the illimitable hope, the unchilled resolution, the inextinguishable faith of youth.

—GEORGE WILLIAM CURTIS.

QUESTIONS AND EXERCISES

1. Clip from any source ten anecdotes and state what truths they may be used to illustrate.

2. Deliver five of these in your own language, without making any application.

3. From the ten, deliver one so as to make the application before telling the anecdote.

4. Deliver another so as to split the application.

5. Deliver another so as to make the application after the narration.

6. Deliver another in such a way as to make a specific application needless.

7. Give three ways of introducing an anecdote, by saying where you heard it, etc.

8. Deliver an illustration that is not strictly an anecdote, in the style of Curtis's speech on page 259.

9. Deliver an address on any public character, using the forms illustrated in this chapter.

10. Deliver an address on some historical event in the same manner.

11. Explain how the sympathies and viewpoint of the speaker will color an anecdote, a biography, or a historical account.

12. Illustrate how the same anecdote, or a section of a historical address, may be given two different effects by personal prejudice.

13. What would be the effect of shifting the viewpoint in the midst of a narration?

14. What is the danger of using too much humor in an address? Too much pathos?

22. Influencing By Suggestion

Sometimes the feeling that a given way of looking at things is undoubtedly correct prevents the mind from thinking at all.... In view of the hindrances which certain kinds or degrees of feeling throw into the way of thinking, it might be inferred that the thinker must suppress the element of feeling in the inner life. No greater mistake could be made. If the Creator endowed man with the power to think, to feel, and to will, these several activities of the mind are not designed to be in conflict, and so long as any one of them is not perverted or allowed to run to excess, it necessarily aids and strengthens the others in their normal functions.

—NATHAN C. SCHAEFFER, *Thinking and Learning to Think.*

When we weigh, compare, and decide upon the value of any given ideas, we reason; when an idea produces in us an opinion or an action, without first being subjected to deliberation, we are moved by suggestion.

Man was formerly thought to be a reasoning animal, basing his actions on the conclusions of natural logic. It was supposed that before forming an opinion or deciding on a course of conduct he weighed at least some of the reasons for and against the matter, and performed a more or less simple process of reasoning. But modern research has shown that quite the opposite is true. Most of our opinions and actions are not based upon conscious reasoning, but are the result of suggestion. In fact, some authorities declare that an act of pure reasoning is very rare in the average mind. Momentous decisions are made, far–reaching actions are determined upon, primarily by the force of suggestion.

Notice that word "primarily," for simple thought, and even mature reasoning, often follows a suggestion accepted in the mind, and the thinker fondly supposes that his conclusion is from first to last based on cold logic.

The Basis of Suggestion

We must think of suggestion both as an effect and as a cause. Considered as an effect, or objectively, there must be something in the hearer that predisposes him to receive suggestion; considered as a cause, or subjectively, there must be some methods by which the speaker can move upon that particularly susceptible attitude of the hearer. How to do this honestly and fairly is our problem—to do it dishonestly and trickily, to use suggestion to bring about conviction and action without a basis of right and truth and in a bad cause, is to assume the terrible responsibility that must fall on the champion of error. Jesus scorned not to use suggestion so that he might move men to their benefit, but every vicious trickster has adopted the same means to reach base ends. Therefore honest men will examine well into their motives and into the truth of their cause, before seeking to influence men by suggestion.

Three fundamental conditions make us all susceptive to suggestion:

We naturally respect authority. In every mind this is only a question of degree, ranging from the subject who is easily hypnotized to the stubborn mind that fortifies itself the more strongly with every assault upon its opinion. The latter type is almost immune to suggestion.

One of the singular things about suggestion is that it is rarely a fixed quantity. The mind that is receptive to the authority of a certain person may prove inflexible to another; moods and environments that produce hypnosis readily in one instance may be entirely inoperative in another; and some minds can scarcely ever be thus moved. We do know, however, that the feeling of the subject that authority—influence, power, domination, control, whatever you wish to call it—lies in the person of the suggester, is the basis of all suggestion.

The extreme force of this influence is demonstrated in hypnotism. The hypnotic subject is told that he is in the water; he accepts the statement as true and makes swimming motions. He is told that a band is marching down the street, playing "The Star Spangled Banner;" he declares he hears the music, arises and stands with head bared.

In the same way some speakers are able to achieve a modified hypnotic effect upon their audiences. The hearers will applaud measures and ideas which, after individual reflection, they will repudiate unless such reflection brings the conviction that the first impression is correct.

A second important principle is that *our feelings, thoughts and wills tend to follow the line of least resistance.* Once open the mind to the sway of one feeling and it requires a greater power of feeling, thought, or will—or even all three—to unseat it. Our feelings influence our judgments and volitions much more than we care to admit. So true is this that it is a superhuman task to get an audience to reason fairly on a subject on which it feels deeply, and when this result is accomplished the success becomes noteworthy, as in the case of Henry Ward Beecher's Liverpool speech. Emotional ideas once accepted are soon cherished, and finally become our very inmost selves. Attitudes based on feelings alone are prejudices.

What is true of our feelings, in this respect, applies to our ideas: All thoughts that enter the mind tend to be accepted as truth unless a stronger and contradictory thought arises.

The speaker skilled in moving men to action manages to dominate the minds of his audience with his thoughts by subtly prohibiting the entertaining of ideas hostile to his own. Most of us are captured by the latest strong attack, and if we can be induced to act while under the stress of that last insistent thought, we lose sight of counter influences. The fact is that almost all our decisions—if they involve thought at all—are of this sort: At the moment of decision the course of action then under contemplation usurps the attention, and conflicting ideas are dropped out of consideration.

The head of a large publishing house remarked only recently that ninety per cent of the people who bought books by subscription never read them. They buy because the salesman presents his wares so skillfully that every consideration but the attractiveness of the book drops out of the mind, and that thought prompts action. *Every* idea that enters the mind will result in action unless a contradictory thought arises to prohibit it. Think of singing the musical scale and it will result in your singing it unless the counter–thought of its futility or absurdity inhibits your action. If you bandage and "doctor" a horse's foot, he will go lame. You cannot think of swallowing, without the muscles used in that process being affected. You cannot think of saying "hello," without a slight movement of the muscles of speech. To warn children that they should not put beans up their noses is the surest method of getting them to do it. Every thought called up in the mind of your audience will work either for or against you. Thoughts are not dead matter; they radiate dynamic energy—the thoughts all tend to pass into action. "Thought is another name for fate." Dominate your hearers' thoughts, allay all contradictory ideas, and you will sway them as you wish.

Volitions as well as feelings and thoughts tend to follow the line of least resistance. That is what makes habit. Suggest to a man that it is impossible to change his mind and in most cases it becomes more difficult to do so—the exception is the man who naturally jumps to the contrary. Counter suggestion is the only way to reach him. Suggest subtly and persistently that the opinions of those in the audience who are opposed to your views are changing, and it requires an effort of the will—in fact, a summoning of the forces of feeling, thought and will—to stem the tide of change that has subconsciously set in.

But, not only are we moved by authority, and tend toward channels of least resistance: *We are all influenced by our environments*. It is difficult to rise above the sway of a crowd—its enthusiasms and its fears are contagious because they are suggestive. What so many feel, we say to ourselves, must have some basis in truth. Ten times ten makes more than one hundred. Set ten men to speaking to ten audiences of ten men each, and compare the aggregate power of those ten speakers with that of one man addressing one hundred men. The ten speakers may be more logically convincing than the single orator, but the chances are strongly in favor of the one man's reaching a greater total effect, for the hundred men will radiate conviction and resolution as ten small groups could not. We all know the truism about the enthusiasm of numbers. (See the chapter on "Influencing the Crowd.")

Environment controls us unless the contrary is strongly suggested. A gloomy day, in a drab room, sparsely tenanted by listeners, invites platform disaster. Everyone feels it in the air. But let the speaker walk squarely up to the issue and suggest by all his feeling, manner and words that this is going to be a great gathering in every vital sense, and see how the suggestive power of environment recedes before the advance of a more potent suggestion—if such the speaker is able to make it.

Now these three factors—respect for authority, tendency to follow lines of least resistance, and susceptibility to environment—all help to bring the auditor into a state of mind favorable to suggestive influences, but they also react on the speaker, and now we must consider those personally causative, or subjective, forces which enable him to use suggestion effectively.

How the Speaker Can Make Suggestion Effective

We have seen that under the influence of authoritative suggestion the audience is inclined to accept the speaker's assertion without argument and criticism. But the audience is not in this state of mind unless it has implicit confidence in the speaker. If they lack faith in him, question his motives or knowledge, or even object to his manner they will not be moved by his most logical conclusion and will fail to give him a just hearing. *It is all a matter of their confidence in him.* Whether the speaker finds it already in the warm, expectant look of his hearers, or must win to it against opposition or coldness, he must gain that one great vantage point before his suggestions take on power in the hearts of his listeners. Confidence is the mother of Conviction.

Note in the opening of Henry W. Grady's after–dinner speech how he attempted to secure the confidence of his audience. He created a receptive atmosphere by a humorous story; expressed his desire to speak with earnestness and sincerity; acknowledged "the vast interests involved;" deprecated his "untried arm," and professed his humility. Would not such an introduction give you confidence in the speaker, unless you were strongly opposed to him? And even then, would it not partly disarm your antagonism?

Mr. President:—Bidden by your invitation to a discussion of the race problem—forbidden by occasion to make a political speech—I appreciate, in trying to reconcile orders with propriety, the perplexity of the little maid, who, bidden to learn to swim, was yet adjured, "Now, go, my darling; hang your clothes on a hickory limb, and don't go near the water."

The stoutest apostle of the Church, they say, is the missionary, and the missionary, wherever he unfurls his flag, will never find himself in deeper need of unction and address than I, bidden tonight to plant the standard of a Southern Democrat in Boston's banquet hall, and to discuss the problem of the races in the home of Phillips and of Sumner. But, Mr. President, if a purpose to speak in perfect frankness and sincerity; if earnest understanding of the vast interests involved; if a consecrating sense of what disaster may follow further misunder-

standing and estrangement; if these may be counted to steady un-
disciplined speech and to strengthen an untried arm—then, sir, I shall
find the courage to proceed.

Note also Mr. Bryan's attempt to secure the confidence of his audi-
ence in the following introduction to his "Cross of Gold" speech de-
livered before the National Democratic Convention in Chicago, 1896.
He asserts his own inability to oppose the "distinguished gentleman;"
he maintains the holiness of his cause; and he declares that he will
speak in the interest of humanity—well knowing that humanity is likely
to have confidence in the champion of their rights. This introduction
completely dominated the audience, and the speech made Mr. Bryan
famous.

Mr. Chairman and Gentlemen of the Convention: I would be presump-
tuous indeed to present myself against the distinguished gentlemen
to whom you have listened if this were a mere measuring of abilities;
but this is not a contest between persons. The humblest citizen in all
the land, when clad in the armor of a righteous cause, is stronger than
all the hosts of error. I come to speak to you in defense of a cause as
holy as the cause of liberty—the cause of humanity.

Some speakers are able to beget confidence by their very manner,
while others can not.

To secure confidence, be confident. How can you expect others to
accept a message in which you lack, or seem to lack, faith yourself?
Confidence is as contagious as disease. Napoleon rebuked an officer
for using the word "impossible" in his presence. The speaker who will
entertain no idea of defeat begets in his hearers the idea of his victory.
Lady Macbeth was so confident of success that Macbeth changed his
mind about undertaking the assassination. Columbus was so certain
in his mission that Queen Isabella pawned her jewels to finance his
expedition. Assert your message with implicit assurance, and your own
belief will act as so much gunpowder to drive it home.

Advertisers have long utilized this principle. "The machine you will
eventually buy," "Ask the man who owns one," "Has the strength of
Gibraltar," are publicity slogans so full of confidence that they give
birth to confidence in the mind of the reader.

It should—but may not!—go without saying that confidence must have a solid ground of merit or there will be a ridiculous crash. It is all very well for the "spellbinder" to claim all the precincts—the official count is just ahead. The reaction against over–confidence and over–suggestion ought to warn those whose chief asset is mere bluff.

A short time ago a speaker arose in a public–speaking club and asserted that grass would spring from wood–ashes sprinkled over the soil, without the aid of seed. This idea was greeted with a laugh, but the speaker was so sure of his position that he reiterated the statement forcefully several times and cited his own personal experience as proof. One of the most intelligent men in the audience, who at first had derided the idea, at length came to believe in it. When asked the reason for his sudden change of attitude, he replied: "Because the speaker is so confident." In fact, he was so confident that it took a letter from the U.S. Department of Agriculture to dislodge his error.

If by a speaker's confidence, intelligent men can be made to believe such preposterous theories as this where will the power of self–reliance cease when plausible propositions are under consideration, advanced with all the power of convincing speech?

Note the utter assurance in these selections:

I know not what course others may take, but as for me give me liberty or give me death.

—PATRICK HENRY.

I ne'er will ask ye quarter, and I ne'er will be your slave;
But I'll swim the sea of slaughter, till I sink beneath its wave.

—PATTEN.

Come one, come all. This rock shall fly
From its firm base as soon as I.

—SIR WALTER SCOTT.

INVICTUS

Out of the night that covers me,
Black as the pit from pole to pole,

I thank whatever Gods may be
For my unconquerable soul.

In the fell clutch of circumstance
I have not winced nor cried aloud;
Under the bludgeonings of chance
My head is bloody, but unbowed.

Beyond this place of wrath and tears
Looms but the Horror of the shade,
And yet the menace of the years
Finds and shall find me unafraid.

It matters not how strait the gate,
How charged with punishments the scroll,
I am the master of my fate;
I am the captain of my soul.

—WILLIAM ERNEST HENLEY.

Authority is a factor in suggestion. We generally accept as truth, and without criticism, the words of an authority. When he speaks, contradictory ideas rarely arise in the mind to inhibit the action he suggests. A judge of the Supreme Court has the power of his words multiplied by the virtue of his position. The ideas of the U.S. Commissioner of Immigration on his subject are much more effective and powerful than those of a soap manufacturer, though the latter may be an able economist.

This principle also has been used in advertising. We are told that the physicians to two Kings have recommended Sanatogen. We are informed that the largest bank in America, Tiffany and Co., and The State, War, and Navy Departments, all use the Encyclopedia Britannica. The shrewd promoter gives stock in his company to influential bankers or business men in the community in order that he may use their examples as a selling argument.

If you wish to influence your audience through suggestion, if you would have your statements accepted without criticism or argument, you should appear in the light of an authority—and *be* one. Ignorance and credulity will remain unchanged unless the suggestion of authority be followed promptly by facts. Don't claim authority unless you carry your license in your pocket. Let reason support the position that suggestion has assumed.

Advertising will help to establish your reputation—it is "up to you" to maintain it. One speaker found that his reputation as a magazine writer was a splendid asset as a speaker. Mr. Bryan's publicity, gained by three nominations for the presidency and his position as Secretary of State, helps him to command large sums as a speaker. But—back of it all, he *is* a great speaker. Newspaper announcements, all kinds of advertising, formality, impressive introductions, all have a capital effect on the attitude of the audience. But how ridiculous are all these if a toy pistol is advertised as a sixteen–inch gun!

Note how authority is used in the following to support the strength of the speaker's appeal:

Professor Alfred Russell Wallace has just celebrated his 90th birthday. Sharing with Charles Darwin the honor of discovering evolution, Professor Wallace has lately received many and signal honors from scientific societies. At the dinner given him in London his address was largely made up of reminiscences. He reviewed the progress of civilization during the last century and made a series of brilliant and startling contrasts between the England of 1813 and the world of 1913. He affirmed that our progress is only seeming and not real. Professor Wallace insists that the painters, the sculptors, the architects of Athens and Rome were so superior to the modern men that the very fragments of their marbles and temples are the despair of the present day artists. He tells us that man has improved his telescope and spectacles, but that he is losing his eyesight; that man is improving his looms, but stiffening his fingers; improving his automobile and his locomotive, but losing his legs; improving his foods, but losing his digestion. He adds that the modern white slave traffic, orphan asylums, and tenement house life in factory towns, make a black page in the history of the twentieth century.

Professor Wallace's views are reinforced by the report of the commission of Parliament on the causes of the deterioration of the factory–class people. In our own country Professor Jordan warns us against war, intemperance, overworking, underfeeding of poor children, and disturbs our contentment with his "Harvest of Blood." Professor Jenks is more pessimistic. He thinks that the pace, the climate, and the stress of city life, have broken down the Puritan stock, that in another century our old families will be extinct, and that the flood of immigration means a Niagara of muddy waters fouling the pure springs of American life. In his address in New Haven Professor Kellogg calls the roll of the signs of race degeneracy and tells us that this deterioration even indicates a trend toward race extinct